HEALING SECRETS
FROM THE BIBLE

HEALING SECRETS
FROM THE BIBLE

———————◆———————

GOD WANTS US TO BE HEALTHY,
AND THE BIBLE TELLS US HOW.

by

Dr. Patrick Quillin, PhD,RD,CNS

published by

N T P

The Nutrition Times Press, Inc.
Tulsa

Other books by Patrick Quillin, PhD, RD, CNS

Beating Cancer with Nutrition, 1994
Adjuvant Nutrition in Cancer Treatment, 1993
The Wisdom of Amish Folk Medicine, 1993
Safe Eating, 1990
The La Costa Book of Nutrition, 1987
Healing Nutrients, 1987
The La Costa Prescription for Longer Life, 1985

© **1996 Patrick Quillin**
ISBN 0-9638372-1-4

Selected illustrations by Noreen Quillin & Lynn Marcoe

Printed in the United States of America

How to order:
Quantity discounts are available from:

The Nutrition Times Press, Inc.
Box 700512, Tulsa, OK 74170-0512
Telephone 918-495-1137.

On your letterhead, include information concerning the intended use of the books and the number of books you wish to purchase.

CONTENTS

DEDICATION

To God and His Son Jesus Christ go all the glory. Thank you for allowing me to be an inspired instrument of your love.

ACKNOWLEDGEMENTS

For the thousands of brilliant and persistent Biblical scholars who dedicated their lives to better understanding the Word of God. With their insight, concordances, notes, maps, and computer programs; the Bible has become an even more approachable and immediately relevant guide to living a longer and better life, thus fulfilling the words of Jesus:

I have come that they may have life, and have it to the full. **John10:10**

IMPORTANT NOTICE

CHAPTER 1

GOD WANTS YOU TO BE HEALTHY

MY PEOPLE ARE DESTROYED FROM LACK OF KNOWLEDGE (Hosea 4:6)

illions of good Christians suffer unnecessarily with poor health and die prematurely. Why? Because we are not following the basic principles of health that are taught in the Bible.

We slice, dice, chop, blend, hydrogenate, refine, and dismember God's food until there is precious little nourishment left in it. Through years of neglect, we turn bodies that are built for activity into bodies that can barely get off the couch. We pollute our food, air, and water supply with a frightening array of manmade poisons. We subject ourselves to an unending parade of stressful events on TV and movies.

Then, when our starving and poorly maintained bodies begin to breakdown, we use potent drugs to subdue the symptoms of the illness, rather than dealing with the underlying causes of the disease. Our prideful and arrogant medical system has gone well beyond the prudent use of God-given intelligence for healing--we repeatedly violate the body with drugs and surgery when prayer, rest, and good food are often the needed remedies.

God wants you to be healthy. Throughout the Bible, there are numerous references to God's love for His people.

John 10:10 *I have come that they may have life, and have it to the full.*

John 3:16 *For God so loved the world, that he gave his only begotten Son, that whosoever believeth in him should not perish, but have everlasting life.*

John 15:11 *I have told you this so that my joy may be in you and that your joy may be complete.*

Matthew 7:7 *Ask and it will be given to you; seek and you will find; knock and the door will be opened to you.*

1Corinthians .2:9 *However, as it is written: "No eye has seen, no ear has heard, no mind has conceived what God has prepared for those who love him"*

Luke 12:32 *Do not be afraid, little flock, for your Father has been pleased to give you the kingdom.*

The New Testament is, indeed, a "good news" book. One of the major focal points of Jesus's ministry was to heal the sick and even raise the dead.

Matthew 11:5 *The blind receive sight, the lame walk, those who have leprosy are cured, the deaf hear, the dead are raised, and the good news is preached to the poor.*

Many people undergo painful, expensive, and debilitating back surgery when all they needed was some chiropractic manipulation and some exercises to strengthen the region. Many people undergo open heart bypass surgery, which has been proven to offer no life extension, when they merely needed to change their lifestyle to clear out their arteries for good. Many people undergo surgery for carpal tunnel syndrome (a painful condition in the wrist) when vitamin B-6 cures 97% of these people. Many arthritis sufferers take dangerous steroid drugs for decades to subdue the swelling when fish oil and a diet to eliminate food allergens could cure the problem. Many people stagger around with no energy or ability to concentrate when a little magnesium and ginseng could give them a much more enjoyable and productive life. These are just a few examples of the safe, inexpensive, and effective healing principles that use God's methods of nourishing our own ability to heal within, rather than jamming symptoms with drugs and surgery. For those who think that man's food is better than God's food and that man's medicine is better than God's medicine there has been a painful lesson.

There is a humorous and very relevant story told of Reverend Jones, who was working in his garden one bright summer day, when along came a parishioner and commented: "My, my Reverend, doesn't God make a nice garden?" And the Reverend replied: "Yes, but you should have seen it before I got here." The point is, God does His work, and we are expected to do our work. This Junior (man) and Senior (God) partnership (2Cor. 6:1, 1Cor. 3:9) works out to bring exuberant health and long life. Could it be that much of the suffering, illness, tears, pain, and early death are because we are not doing our part?

We tamper with the human body like a 10 year old boy working on a new Ferrari--we really don't know what we are doing and oftentimes do more harm than good. We violate all the principles of health taught in the Bible. Then, when we get sick, we look pleadingly to the skies and ask God: "Why me?" Perhaps our health problems are self-inflicted because we are not following God's word.

1John 3:22 *and receive from him anything we ask, because we obey his commands and do what pleases Him.*

An old country slogan goes: "God feeds all the birds, but He doesn't throw the food into their nest—the birds have to go get it." We have the potential of being vibrantly healthy, yet we have to earn it through our own lifestyle practices. Many Christians are like the person standing on a ledge of a tall building, saying "God, I am going to jump off this roof top and I want you to repeal the laws of gravity and save me." God can do that, but more likely that person will go splat on the pavement below. When tempted by the devil during His forty days in the desert, even Jesus did not "step off the cliff," which He could have done.

> Matthew 4:1-7 *If you are the Son of God,"* *he said, "throw yourself down. For it is written: "'He will command his angels concerning you, and they will lift you up in their hands, so that you will not strike your foot against a stone." Jesus answered him, "It is also written: 'Do not put the Lord your God to the test."*

With all the best of intentions, too many Christians are, literally, stepping off the cliff; expecting God to repeal the laws of gravity and biochemistry which were created by God. It doesn't work that way. Even Jesus, the Son of God, ate good food. Jesus fed the multitudes with fish and barley loaves, not with pizza and soft drinks—which He could have done.

God wants you to live a long and exuberant life. If you are still here on earth reading this book, then you have a valuable "mission" to accomplish. But you cannot enjoy life, as God intended, nor accomplish your mission if your body wears out too soon.

True story. Jack LaLanne and Norman Vincent Peale were having lunch one day, when Dr. Peale asked Jack, "Why are you so obsessed with fitness?". To which Jack replied, "Let me just bend your thumb back in a painful position and let's keep talking." Dr. Peale protested, but tried to continue the conversation. Eventually, Dr. Peale pleaded, "Jack!! That hurts!! What is your point??" The fitness guru responded, "If you don't feel good, then nothing else matters!" Health is very important!!

Personal Profile

LT was a retired widow with advanced painful rheumatoid arthritis. For many years, she had been using aspirin to dull the pain; yet the aspirin eventually resulted in a bleeding stomach ulcer and she had to discontinue its use. Her physician started giving her injections of cortisone to ease the swelling in her joints, but the side effects included reduced immune functions, which brought on common vaginal yeast infections, frequent urination, irregular heartbeat, and a "moon" face development. She came to me asking for help.

I recommended a program to detect her food allergies; which involves eating a hypoallergenic diet of lamb, turkey, rice, pears, apples, carrots, and tea for 4 days; followed by adding common allergy-causing foods one at a time. We found out quickly that she reacted to milk products, corn, peanuts, and lard. By eliminating these foods from her diet, she stopped bringing in foods that were causing the constant irritation in her joints. I also put her on a broad spectrum vitamin and mineral supplement, vitamin C, fish oil, bee pollen, and lots of clean water. Her pain subsided within 2 weeks and within 2 months her arthritis had diminished enough that she was able to resume a full and vigorous life of walking and gardening which she loved so much.

CARING FOR YOUR "TEMPLE OF THE SOUL"

1Corinthians 6:19 *Do you not know that your body is a temple of the Holy Spirit, who is in you, whom you have received from God?*

Many of us are not properly caring for this "temple of the Holy Spirit". For some of us, at the rate we are going, that "temple" is soon going to become a "cathedral". The Old Testament tells us that many of God's people lived to a very advanced age, some to 900 years (Gen 5:5 & 27). Older women were fertile and older men were virile (Gen 21:1-8). Moses died at the age of 120, yet "his eyes were not weak nor his strength gone." (Deut. 34:7)

In the past 30 years, scientists have been accumulating data which proves the merits of the Biblical diet and lifestyle. We are created by God to have certain physical requirements. If we do not meet these needs, then the body does not function well. After years of struggling to perform in spite of poor conditions, the body eventually gives out in disease and early death. But don't blame God. God gave us free will to make our own choices in life.

2Corinthians 3:17 *"Now the Lord is the Spirit, and where the Spirit of the Lord is, there is freedom."*

Yet how many of us misuse our freedom and choose the wrong foods and the wrong lifestyle?

1Corinthians 8:9 *"Be careful, however, that the exercise of your freedom does not become a stumbling block to the weak."*

More Christians suffer from lack of education than inspiration. Too few of us know the guidelines provided in Scripture to nourish the mind and body toward a zesty and fulfilling 80 to 120 years of life. We assume that by giving thanks over the food, God will bless it to nourish our bodies. But when we take God's nourishing food, then strip it of any vestige of nourishment; giving thanks will not turn that adulterated and bankrupt food into something nourishing. By heeding the wisdom in the Bible, we can elevate ourselves out of the routine illnesses that plague Americans.

Joshua 1:7 *Be strong and very courageous. Be careful to obey all the law my servant Moses gave you; do not turn from it to the right or to the left, that you may be successful wherever you go.*

FOOD AS A COVENANT WITH GOD

In Abraham's times, food was a visible means of knowing that there is a God. Plants provided all of the medicines, most of the food, most of the clothing, dyes for painting and writing, and more. Animals provided food, a unique means of converting unproductive shrub land into high quality protein, protection, transportation, hunting companions, clothing and shelter from the hides, and more. All too often, ancient people became so enamored with the miraculous life-giving properties of plants and animals that they worshipped these false idols.

Thanksgiving was offered at meal time because food was the intimate link with God, a sign of God's generosity, a symbol of God's miraculous power. Jesus was represented in the symbol of a fish. Jesus converted water into wine for His first miracle. Jesus used bread and wine in the Passover Feast as symbols of His Body and Blood to be sacrificed at Calvary.

Mark 14:22. *While they were eating, Jesus took bread, gave thanks and broke it, and gave it to his disciples, saying, "Take it; this is my body. This is my blood of the covenant, which is poured out for many."*

Food was a show of strength, of a covenant between God and His people. When the Israelites were wandering the desert, God sent them "manna", which is now widely recognized to be coriander seed.

Exodus 16:31 *The people of Israel called the bread manna. It was white like coriander seed and tasted like wafers made with honey.*

The manna nourished them, but was not part of their previous diet. God used manna as a lesson, to teach the Israelites a lesson.

Deuteronomy 8:3 *He humbled you, causing you to hunger and then feeding you with manna, which neither you nor your fathers had known, to teach you that man does not live on bread alone but on every word that comes from the mouth of the LORD.*

Today, we look at food as a hedonistic pleasure, something to fill up the hole in the stomach, something to soothe our troubled nerves after a harried day, something to bring back fond memories of happier times. These are all okay. Food should bring pleasure. But when pleasure is the only criteria that we use to chose our food, then we have ignored God's purpose for providing food; which is to nourish the body with essential nutrients found in plants and animals, and to provide a physical connection with a seemingly invisible God.

Modern man takes God's food and heavily sprays it with pesticides, then removes valuable nutrients in the refining stage, then adds questionable agents like salt, fat, sugar, and 2800 different Food and Drug Administration approved food additives. Then we wonder why our health is failing.

OUR HEALTH CARE "ARMAGEDDON" (REV. 16:16)

America spends over $1 trillion each year on what we euphemistically call "health care", which is more "disease maintenance" than anything else. We spend twice the money per capita as any other nation on earth for health care. And our "health state of the union" is less than spectacular:

† 58 million Americans have high blood pressure
† half of us die from heart disease and one fourth from cancer, both diseases were relatively unknown in Abraham's time
† 24 million have insomnia
† 50 million have regular headaches
† 55 billion aspirin consumed yearly
† 9 million alcoholics
† 40% are overweight
† 40 million have mental illness
† 9.6 million older adults each year suffer drug-induced side effects, including 659,000 hospitalizations and 163,000 with memory loss

When the doctor sets a broken bone, he or she does not heal the patient, but rather sets in place the tissue so that God can heal us from within. Same thing happens in stitching up a cut, or when you recovered from your last bout with the flu. The only way you stay well or heal from a health challenge is by nourishing that "God-given life force" within us. When we stop trying to play God and start cooperating within the framework of God's natural biochemical laws, then we will find a quantum leap in our health and improved results at the doctor's office.

America is near the top (worst) in the world for heart disease, cancer, diabetes, mental illness, osteoporosis, and other diseases which were unknown in Abraham's time. We have a worse infant survival record than such undeveloped countries as Venezuela and the Phillipines. Essentially, we have ignored our roots and the commandments from God and have suffered the consequences. But God wants us to be healthy, and the Bible tells us how.

MALNUTRITION IN AMERICA— THE GREAT NUTRITION ROBBERY

Isaiah 55:2 *Why spend money on what is not bread, and your labor on what does not satisfy? Listen, listen to me, and eat what is good, and your soul will delight in the richest of fare.*

America is the most agriculturally productive nation in the history of the world. We grow enough food in this country to feed ourselves, to make half of us overweight, to throw away enough food to feed 50 million people daily, to ship food overseas as a major export, and to store enough food in government surplus bins to feed Americans for a year if all farmers quit today. With so much food available, how can Americans be malnourished? The simple answer is: poor food choices.

People in Western Society

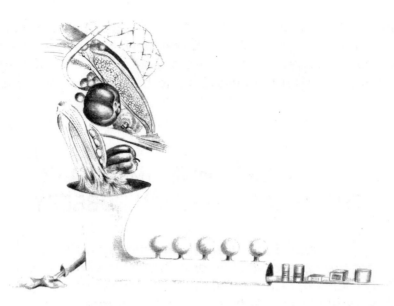

choose their food based upon taste, cost, convenience and psychological gratification—thus ignoring the main reason that we eat, which is to provide our body cells with the raw materials to grow, repair and fuel our bodies. We take God's elegantly designed nutritious foods and:

1. use drugs, hormones, and antibiotics to raise animals faster, while spraying 1.2 billion pounds of pesticides over our food crops

2. fail to properly fertilize the soil with organic matter and trace minerals and allow fields to lie fallow, as was done in Biblical times

3. remove vitamins, minerals, and fiber during extensive food processing

4. add over 2800 Food and Drug Administration approved additives, including salt, fat, sugar, and unsafe food additives, like saccharin and MSG

5. dramatically increase the cost of the food, which compounds the problems for the poor.

The fact is: the nutrients were in that food for a very good reason. God is the ultimate "Engineer" in designing and building the human body and providing us with all of our needs. When we

Malnutrition in typical "healthy" American

average annual consumption of low nutrient foods:

756 doughnuts

60 pounds cakes & cookies

23 gallons ice cream

7 pounds potato chips

22 pounds candy

200 sticks gum

365 servings soda pop

90 pounds fat

134 pounds refined sugar

tamper with the food supply, we usually wreak havoc on the food's nutritional content. The most commonly eaten foods in America are white bread, coffee and hot dogs, which have little to offer the body. Based upon our food abundance and affluence, Americans could be the best nourished nation on record. But we are far from it.

In the late 1930s, Dr. Weston Price, a dentist, and his wife, Monica, who was also a nurse, were intrigued by the possible link between diet and health. In true "Indiana Jones" adventure some fashion, they travelled the world logging over 100,000 miles on primitive aircraft to investigate 17 different cultures. What they found was startling to scientists then, but had already been written in the Bible thousands of years ago. The more refined (read: adulterated) the food supply, the worse the health of the people. Those people who ate their God-given diet had excellent health, teeth structure, energy, and appearance. Those who deviated from their God-given diet suffered everything from mild symptoms, such as acne, skin and hair problems, and poor dental formation to the severest forms of mental retardation and even paralysis.

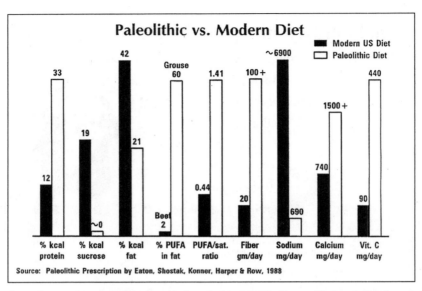

Paleolithic vs. Modern Diet

Source: Paleolithic Prescription by Eaton, Shostak, Konner, Harper & Row, 1988

Another group of researchers in 1988 from Emory University in Atlanta followed up on Dr. Price's work and found similar results. They stated that the "paleolithic" diet was very different from our current refined diet, and that difference may contribute to many of our ailments.[2] Our ancestors from Abraham's time, the hunter and gatherers, ate a superior diet and enjoyed superior health. See the chart above which compares our modern diet to that of Abraham's era.

Overwhelming evidence from government surveys of 200,000 Americans and numerous respected universities shows that many Americans are low in their intake of:

   † VITAMINS: A, D, E, C, B-6, riboflavin, folacin, pantothenic acid

   † MINERALS: calcium, potassium, magnesium, zinc, iron, chromium, selenium; and possibly molybdenum and vanadium.

   † MACRONUTRIENTS: fiber, complex carbohydrates, plant protein, special fatty acids (EPA, GLA, ALA), clean water

Meanwhile, we also eat alarmingly high amounts of: fat, salt, sugar, cholesterol, alcohol, caffeine, food additives and toxins.

This combination of too much of the wrong things along with

not enough of the right things has created epidemic proportions of degenerative diseases in this country. The Surgeon General, Department of Health and Human Services, Center for Disease Control, National Academy of Sciences, American Medical Association, American Dietetic Assocation, and most other major public health agencies agree that diet is a major contributor to our most common health problems, including cancer and heart disease.

The typical American diet is high in fat while being low in fiber and vegetables. "Meat, potatoes, and gravy" is what many of my cancer patients lived on for decades. Data collected by the United States Department of Agriculture from over 11,000 Americans showed that on any given day:

† 41 percent did not eat any fruit

† 82 percent did not eat cruciferous vegetables

† 72 percent did not eat vitamin C-rich fruits or vegetables

† 80 percent did not eat vitamin A-rich fruits or vegetables

† 84 percent did not eat high fiber grain food, like bread or cereal

The human body is incredibly resilient, which sometimes works to our disadvantage. No one dies on the first cigarette inhaled, or the first drunken evening, or the first decade of unhealthy eating. We misconstrue the fact that we survived this ordeal to mean we can do it forever. Not so. Malnutrition can be blatant, as the starving babies in third world countries. Malnutrition can also be much more subtle; first bringing the vague symptoms of chronic fatigue, constipation, mood swings, poor wound recovery, and frequent colds; followed by a decade of struggling with incontinence, poor memory, pain in the chest, poor digestion, and visual problems. Malnutrition in America is a progressive and silent saboteur from within the body, not an instant knockout punch.

It was the Framingham study done at Harvard University that proclaimed: "Our way of life is related to our way of death." While many Americans are overfed, the majority are also poorly nourished. The typical American, statistically speaking, is overweight, has six colds per year, is regularly plagued with lethargy, mild depression, and constipation, gets dentures by age 45, begins a marked decline in function and vitality by age 50, and dies in their 60s or 70s from heart disease or cancer. Another scientist has stated the problem more bluntly: "We are digging our graves with our teeth."

USE AND ABUSE OF MODERN MEDICINE

Proverbs16:18 *Pride goes before destruction, a haughty spirit before a fall.*

America has the most expensive and technologically advanced health care system in the world. For acute critical care, no medical system in the world can match ours. Yet, oftentimes we fight the symptoms of degenerative diseases with drugs and surgery in a futile losing battle, when the real answer to the patient's health problems might have been something as simple as diet improvement, or gentle herbal healers, or a sympathetic ear. Think of a sink overflowing with a mess of water all over the floor. Our medical system spends an incredible amount of time

and money trying to wipe up the mess on the floor when the easiest solution is to turn off the faucet that produces the diseases.

Dr. Christiaan Barnard, the pioneering heart transplant surgeon, claims that the greatest progress in health care in the last 500 years came from, not a drug or surgical procedure, but the invention of the indoor flushing toilet, thus eliminating the many plagues caused by contaminated water supplies. The World Health Organization has reported that 70% of the world's population uses herbs and foods as their primary healing instruments, many of which are in jeopardy of being lost as the tropical rain forests disappear. Hippocrates, the Greek father of modern medicine told us 2400 years ago "Let food be your medicine and medicine be your food." and "...in nature there is strength."

Throughout the world and recorded history, natural healing agents were the main tools of the physician, with herbs serving as the favored medicines. Avicenna was an Arab herbalist who lived in the 11th century and travelled extensively throughout the known world to catalog the medical uses of herbs. He eventually wrote 100 books on this subject, culminating in his 1 million word tome: CANON OF MEDICINE. This book was considered a standard for medical education throughout Europe and Asia until the 17th century.

Genesis1:30 *And to all the beasts of the earth and all the birds of the air and all the creatures that move on the ground—everything that has the breath of life in it—I give every green plant for food." And it was so.*

The big shift in medical outlook began with a Swiss physician, Theophrastus von Hohenheim, who became discontent in the early 16th century with his training and began wandering Europe. While in the mines in Italy, Hohenheim was intrigued by the refining of minerals. He took this knowledge and began using mercury to treat his patients. He further dabbled in the use of strong minerals for medicines. His methods were widely criticized and he died after being tossed from a window by his adversaries while only 50 years old.

Around 1850, a French chemist, Louis Pasteur, found that heat could kill the tiny organisms that caused infections. Pasteur also worked on weakening the bacteria and injecting them into healthy people to prevent the disease—a process we now accept widely as vaccination. In 1910, Abraham Flexner wrote his famous report, *MEDICAL EDUCATION IN THE UNITED STATES AND CANADA*, which highly criticized all forms of healing except allopathy, which uses strong drugs to treat conditions. Practitioners of herbal or naturopathic medicine were ushered out of town, and the era of monopoly control by drug and surgery-oriented medical doctors began.

By 1928, Alexander Fleming had taken penicillin from bread mold and injected it into a patient with an infection. The recovery process was astoundingly quick and the era of antibiotics was born. By the end of World War II, the development of chemicals were coming faster than they could be cataloged or tested for safety. The chemical age was born, and with it came the mixed blessings of miracle materials and the immoral contamination of God's green earth. In the 1950s, Jonas Salk brought us the polio vacccine, and helped to end one of the worst scourges of mankind.

There is a difference between using our knowledge to improve our lot and abusing our knowledge through ego to worsen our lot. Drugs and surgery have their places in the healing arts, especially as short term fixes to get an acutely ill patient through a crisis phase. There are times when no other form of healing will work. But when we rely on these invasive therapies to heal a problem which can only be healed by following God's laws, we end up worse off. We need to be more restrained with medical therapies and more liberal with God's healing therapies. The intelligent combination would leave us with astoundingly good health. Below, I have listed steps to take when a health problem arises. First, try the "cell restoration" therapies of God, and only as a last resort should we use the symptom-treating therapies of drugs and surgery.

I have worked with many patients who were defying all of God's laws: poor food, smoking, no exercise, stress, no prayer, and a body loaded with toxins. Without a thought for changing

INTERVENTION STRATEGIES FOR PREVENTION AND CURE OF DISEASE	
1st line strategies, cell restoration, non-invasive	2nd line strategies, symptom relief, invasive
psycho-spiritual **detoxification** **diet-food** **nutrition concentrates:** vitamins, minerals, amino acids, fatty acids, food extracts, phytochemicals, botanicals **organ replacement therapy:** DHEA (adrenals), thyroxin (thyroid), hydrochloric acid (stomach), enzymes (pancreas), insulin (pancreas beta cells) **body maintenance:** chiropractic manipulation, acupressure/puncture, reflexology, shoe arch, bed support **exercise** **other:** magnets, aroma therapy, homeopathy, etc.	**drugs** **surgery** **chemotherapy (xenobiotics)** **radiation** **hyperthermia** **biological therapies** **others**

this semi-suicidal lifestyle, the doctor will put the patient on an endless array of prescription drugs, which all have dastardly side effects, until the patient eventually develops a really serious disease, like cancer. We arrogantly assume that drugs can reverse the abuse caused by decades of poor nutrition and toxic burden. We are not respecting God's laws of nature.

◆

MY PERSONAL STORY—RE-DISCOVERING GOD

I was raised in an Irish, Catholic home with parents, priests, nuns, and teachers who did their best. Yet, I was brought up amidst fear, guilt, manipulation, and hypocrisy. I did what I thought it took to achieve peace of mind. I followed the rules of the Catholic church, was an altar boy, studied hard and went to the University of Notre Dame. As a student, we dissected dead animals, depressing existentialist writings, and the Word of God. For many reasons, I was miserable and did not return for my junior year of college, but instead travelled and worked at various trades. My dying faith went into a long coma.

Eventually, I realized my interests in nutrition. I went back to college at San Diego State University and found the wonders of biology to be very intriguing. I found out that several studies had been published showing how poor nutrition was a primary factor that ignited many diseases among Americans. I once believed in a vindictive God who randomly struck His people with devastating diseases and could care less about their misery. This misconception was beginning to melt as the facts about self-induced diseases surfaced. I saw harmony and beauty in how God orchestrated life, how intricately the human body works, how God has provided us with the "raw materials" in food to sustain good health, and how tenacious we are built.

Scientific reports about the benefits of "whole food" (read: God's food) began to confirm a suspicion I was developing: "God wants us to be healthy". Though science has evolved to an advanced state, even my brightest professors could not explain how a single-celled fertilized human egg becomes a complex 50 trillion celled functional human within a brief 9 months. No one could fully explain cell differentiation, or enzyme kinetics, or "spontaneous regression of cancer", or the aging process. I began developing a deep appreciation for God's ability to orchestrate life. As laboratory equipment kept getting more sophisticated, scientists continued finding more therapeutic ingredients in God's food. I went back to the Scripture that I had long ago read, but this time the Holy Spirit brought life, love, and meaning to the words of the Bible.

I came to know the Word of God and the love of His Son, Jesus Christ. And it was the Divinely orchestrated healing power of nutrition that renewed my interest in the Bible. What I now see in the Bible is a manual for living a full, healthy, and exuberant life in body, mind, and spirit. The Bible is the complete guide for earning a good living, working with others, marrying the right mate, raising children, staying healthy, solving problems, and dying in peace knowing that we will be with God in the afterlife. Everything in the Bible is true, including the precepts on health and eating. God wants you to be healthy, yet for every promise from God, there is a condition. You must follow God's Biblical laws of healing in order to claim your Divine inheritance of good health and long life.

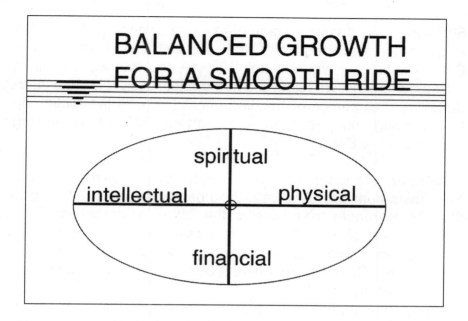

BALANCED GROWTH FOR A SMOOTH RIDE

spiritual

intellectual   physical

financial

BALANCED GROWTH: SPIRITUAL, INTELLECTUAL, PHYSICAL, FINANCIAL

The headlines are full of stories about sports and entertainment celebrities who developed financially, but in no other ways. These people end up very unhappy or in some early tragic death, like Elvis. Other people might develop only in their intellectual path, and end up equally unhappy. We need balanced growth for a "smooth ride" in life. Note the above illustration. If a wheel is lopsided, it does not turn well. If we develop in all aspects of our life, then we are developing our talents in a balanced fashion, as God wants us to.

SCRIPTURE & THE HEALING ARTS

More than coincidentally, the Bible and modern science have independently developed a collection of "lifestyle" influences on health, including: nutrition, exercise, attitude, physical environment (light, toxins & bacteria), and body maintenance.

Not that God needs anyone to endorse His words found in

Scripture, but I do find it comforting when science and the Bible arrive at the same endpoint: that the diet and lifestyle of our Biblical ancestors was enviably healthy and that we can claim the same health if we follow the same rules. Below are the inter-disciplinary examples of "healing principles from the Bible". In the following chapters, there will be more examples of healing foods from the Bible.

Stress. Thousands of years ago, authors of the Old and New Testament told us to relax and be at peace. In addition to the 128 references to "rejoice" in the Bible, Jesus told us:

> John 14:27 *Peace I leave with you; my peace I give you. I do not give to you as the world gives. Do not let your hearts be troubled and do not be afraid.*

For centuries, the country doctor has known the influence of stress on health. Yet only recently have scientists been able to measure and weigh the chemicals produced by the brain during stress. Endorphins are "rivers of pleasure" that flow when we are happy, such as the expression "whatever melts your butter." Catecholamines are the "rivers of stress" that flow when our car gets stuck on a railroad track, or our boss wants us to do some-thing that cannot be done. Through both animal and human studies, scientists know that when these stress hormones flow too much, we get:

† elevated blood pressure; hypertension is the most common condition in America

† erosion of the stomach lining, such as ulcers; the most profitable drug in America is Tagamet for ulcers

† shrinkage of the thymus gland, which directs the protective action of our immune system.

The 1990s, more than coincidentally, has become the decade of immune suppressive disorders, with cancer, AIDS, Chronic Fatigue Syndrome, Candida, auto-immune disorders, allergies, Legionnaire's, and Lou Gehrig's disease becoming increasingly prominent.

Drug addicts artificially prod the brain to produce more endorphins, which often leaves drug abusers with "pleasure center burnout"— they have used up today's and tomorrow's endorphins and now cannot feel any pleasure, like rubbing a spot on your skin until it is numb. When we are under stress, such as fear, hate, resentment, sarcasm, too much to do in too little period of time, or low self-esteem; then less endorphins flow and more catecholamines flow.

Philippians 4:6 *Do not be anxious about anything, but in everything, by prayer and petition, with Thanksgiving, present your requests to God. And the peace of God, which transcends all understanding, will guard your hearts and your minds in Christ Jesus.*

Scientists at the National Institutes of Health spent 10 years and many millions of dollars investigating the origin of the number one cause of death in America: heart disease. They found many variables that influenced this disease, including obesity, smoking, sedentary lifestyle, fat, fiber, chromium, and more. But the most predictive risk factor for heart disease was "loneliness"; which is nothing more than a deficiency of love.

1Corinthians 13:13 *And now these three remain: faith, hope and love. But the greatest of these is love.*

Dr. Candace Pert, researcher at the National Institutes of Health who discovered endorphins, tells us that "our mind is a 24 hour pharmacy and is always making chemicals, which are either good or bad for us." Norman Cousins brought notoriety to the field of the "mind-body connection" in his book, *ANATOMY OF AN ILLNESS*, in which he used vitamin C and laughter to heal himself from a painful and untreatable skeletal disorder. His pet theories were later proven at the University of California at Los Angeles. There are personality types that are more at risk for developing cancer or heart disease. Dr. Hans Selye, father of the modern theories on stress, concluded his brilliant scientific career more as an armchair philosopher, telling us to "lean on a Higher Power" to minimize the impact of stress on the body. Stress is one of the more important risk factors that can cause bone demineralization and osteoporosis. And 3,000 years ago the Bible told us:

> Proverbs14:30 *A heart at peace gives life to the body, but envy rots the bones.*

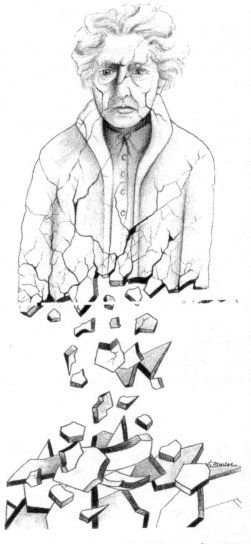

Belief systems. Modern psychologists have found that what we believe at the core of our being, is what will be manifest in our lives. If we think we are losers, then our lives will go accordingly. If we think we are winners, then so be it. If we think that a job is possible, then it will get done. If we think we are destined to be fat, then no diet will be able to help us.

> Proverbs 23:7 *For as he thinketh in his heart, so is he.*

Jesus tells us that a consciousness of love, health, and prosperity will give us a life of abundance, while a consciousness of hate, sickness, and poverty will take everything away.

> Matthew 13:12 *Whoever has will be given more, and he will have an abundance. Whoever does not have, even what he has will be taken from him.*

Dr. Maxwell Maltz, a famous plastic surgeon, coined the term "psycho-cybernetics", meaning that we are goal-oriented creatures. Once we have an image firmly entrenched in our sub-conscious, we will spend all of our energies making the image come true--for better or for worse. Once we understand this simple but powerful principle, we can change our beliefs and change our lives for the better.

> 2Peter 1:4 *Through these He has given us his very great and precious promises, so that through them you may participate in the divine nature...*

> Luke17:21 *...because the kingdom of God is within you."*

> Matthew 8:13 *Then Jesus said to the centurion, "Go! It will be done just as you believed it would." And his servant was healed at that very hour.*

Drunkenness. There are 38 warnings against drunkenness in the Bible. Wine was the downfall of many good people in ancient times, but the real hazard came with distilled spirits which concentrate the alcohol content by 4 to 6 fold. In the 16th century, when gin was first introduced to Europe, England was nearly brought to its knees with the damage done to society from alcohol abuse. In the 1920's, unsuccessful efforts were made to ban alcohol during the Prohibition era in America.

Scientists now tell us that alcohol abuse causes damage to the liver, cancer, heart disease, hypoglycemia (low blood sugar), birth defects, marital breakups, spousal abuse, and at least half of all car and boating accidents. And the first authority to caution against drunkenness was God.

> Proverbs 20:1 *Wine is a mocker and beer a brawler; whoever is led astray by them is not wise.*

Then we come to the subject of moderate wine use versus alcohol abuse. Jesus's first miracle was to turn water into wine for a group of people who were already on the third day of a wedding bash. Jesus drank wine often, including as part of the Passover ritual in which He spoke of wine as a symbol of His blood. There are 222 references to wine in the Bible, including some which praise its value.

1Timothy 5:23 *Stop drinking only water, and use a little wine because of your stomach and your frequent illnesses.*

Interestingly enough, there is an abundance of scientific evidence showing that 1 to 2 glasses of wine daily actually lower the risk for heart disease and gallstones and increase lifespan. This is no contradiction. Small amounts of wine provide "phytochemicals" or substances from red grapes that can help slow down the disease and aging process. Small amounts of alcohol raise the "good cholesterol", HDL.

Yet, abuse of wine or any other liquor is strictly forbidden by God. Women who are pregnant, people prone toward alcoholism, and people operating vehicles and equipment should consider abstinence as their best guidelines on alcohol.

Detoxification. Through our unrestrained and misguided plunge into the modern age of chemistry, America has become the land of toxic wastes. We now dump 90 billion pounds of toxins into our 55,000 garbage dump sites across the country. We add 1.2 billion pounds of pesticides to our fresh produce. The Environmental Protection Agency has stated that 40% of our fresh water is unfit for any use, much less drinking. 50 million Americans live in air that is hazardous for their health. Through lawn herbicides, oven cleaners, home pesticides, and paint cleaners, private homes actually contribute just as much pollutants to the environment as big business and farming.

2Corinthians 7:1 *Since we have these promises, dear friends, let us purify ourselves from everything that contaminates body and spirit, perfecting holiness out of reverence for God.*

Even in a perfectly clean environment, waste products accumulate in our cells as a normal by-product of living. That's why we age. But Americans are exposed to extremely poisonous and non-degradable poisons that create a two fold problem:

1. toxins blunt the immune system, which leaves us open to infections, cancer, and aging

2. toxins bind with our DNA cell blueprints to create cancer and premature aging.

What do we do? We use God's cleansing herbs to purge the system of impurities. Modern herbalists consider hyssop to be one of the more outstanding herbs for detoxification of the colon. While detoxification was important in Abraham's day, it is a crucial issue for us. We need to improve our body's ability to purge both natural and synthetic poisons out of the body through sweat, urine, and feces. We need to seriously limit our intake of toxins: don't smoke, if you drink do so only in moderation, use only the minimum prescription drugs, avoid "recreation" drugs, drink filtered water, breathe clean air. More on this in the A,B,C chapter.

> Psalms 51:7 *Cleanse me with hyssop, and I will be clean; wash me, and I will be whiter than snow.*

Fidelity vs promiscuity. The Bible does not take a frigid or Puritanical viewpoint on sex. In the context of marriage, sex is seen as a beautiful expression of Christ's love for the Church.

> Isaiah 62:5 *As a young man marries a maiden, so will your sons marry you; as a bride groom rejoices over his bride, so will your God rejoice over you.*

Sex feels good, and God intended it to be that way. But He did not intend for us to have sex with everyone. The laws are strict on fidelity to one's mate.

Hebrews 13:4 *Marriage should be honored by all, and the marriage bed kept pure, for God will judge the adulterer and the sexually immoral.*

Today, we know that all sorts of diseases are transmitted through unrestrained sexual contact, from the well known gonorrhea and syphilis, to the new nemesis AIDS, to the common but unpublicized problems with venereal warts and chlamydia. Some venereal diseases not only affect the man and woman, but their offspring, such as blindness in a newborn infant caused by syphilis contact through the mother's birth canal.

Modern science now tells us that promiscuity not only shakes the foundations of a marriage, prevents spiritual bonds from forming between partners, but also is a dangerous "roulette" of infectious diseases. Women who have too many sexual partners too early in life run a higher risk of ovarian cancer. One of the more common cancers in the world is cervical cancer, which can be triggered by the Human Papilloma Virus, which can be spread through sexual contact.

Ezekial 23:29 *They will deal with you in hatred and take away everything you have worked for. They will leave you naked and bare, and the shame of your prostitution will be exposed. Your lewdness and promiscuity*

Exercise. Our bodies are built for activity. Without regular exercise, we build up toxins in the body, allow fat to accumulate in the tissue and arteries, and generally age faster. Exercise is one of the more valuable and inexpensive therapies you can give your body. 90% of Americans suffer from some type of back problem, much of which is due to poor muscle tone. Muscles and cartilage hold the bones together. If the muscles atrophy, then the bones develop problems in alignment.

Proverbs 19:15 *Laziness brings on deep sleep, and the shiftless man goes hungry.*

40% of Americans are overweight. Humans and our domestic pets are the only creatures on earth who suffer from obesity.

Much of this is due to sedentary lifestyle. Bring out the leash to take your dog for a walk and the dog becomes ecstatic. Animals feel better when they exercise. Given a chance, so do humans.

> Exodus 20:9 *Six days you shall labor and do all your work*

A Stanford professor has written a detailed scientific article in which he proposes that "dis-ease likely comes from dis-use of the body". Scientists find that regular exercise helps relieve depression, improves regularity, improves heart muscle tone, lowers body fat, allows people to eat more without getting fat, stabilizes blood sugar, and more.

The Israelites worked very hard as slaves under the Egyptians, yet, the Israelites enjoyed very good health during this period. Women gave birth to healthy children before any midwife could arrive on the scene. I can summarize thousands of scientific studies on exercise in two short phrases:

1. You've got to move it to lose it (weight).

2. Use it or lose it—the body atrophies without exercise.

> Proverbs 6:6 *Go to the ant, you sluggard, consider its ways and be wise.*

> Exodus 2:11 *One day, after Moses had grown up, he went out to where his own people were and watched them at their hard labor.*

Circumcision. Four thousand years ago, Abraham was told to circumcise the young male infants. We now know that circumcision practically eliminates cancer of the penis, since uncircumcised men have over a 100 fold increase in their risk for penile cancer.

> Genesis 17:10 *This is my covenant with you and your descendants after you, the covenant you are to keep: Every male among you shall be circumcised.*

More to come. These are just a few of the examples of scientifically-proven healthy ideas presented in the Bible. You will find many more pearls of Scriptural wisdom in later chapters regarding specific foods to eat and avoid. God designed humans as well as our food supply. God knows what is best for us. If we do not follow the "factory specification diet" then our body's warranty is null and void.

IF GOD REALLY LOVES US, THEN WHY IS THERE SICKNESS?

If we follow the principles taught in the Bible and condensed in this book, 9 out of 10 illnesses would be prevented and most people would live several decades longer. However, some people would get sick in spite of following these truths. Why? Though I am not a theologian and certainly do not have all the answers, my many years of working with sick and dying cancer patients have offered some insight that I would like to share with you. Benefits and insights gained through sickness:

1. **Need to need each other.** By being sick or helping the sick, one gains an incredible appreciation for our inter-connectedness. While many people are reluctant to help a healthy per-

son, few people can resist the need to help a sick person. Helping others teaches us love and our oneness through Christ.
Ephesians 4:25   *Therefore each of you must put off falsehood and speak truthfully to his neighbor, for we are all members of one body.*

2. We learn best from Nature when things go wrong. By studying errors in the body, we better appreciate the astounding majesty of God's creations.   Scientists study the difference between sick and well people and can better understand how we function, thus making it possible to develop gentle cures. In my own health challenges, I have been forced to "seek and you shall find" solutions, which I then have shared with my patients, readers, and others. Through my sickness, others found relief.

3. We learn humility in disease. Nothing is more humbling than to be confined to a bed or wheelchair. "There are no atheists in a foxhole" goes the famous World War I expression. I might add, there are no atheists in a cancer hospital. Sometimes, it takes a life-threatening disease to teach us humility.

4. Better appreciate life when we recognize our mortality. I have learned more about savoring life from my cancer patients than anywhere else. We are all mortal, but we rarely take this into consideration in daily life. People facing a life-threatening illness are forced to examine their priorities in life. Believe me, you don't sweat the small stuff when you have a few months to live; and most of what we sweat is small stuff. We can all learn a lesson in savoring life from sick people.

5. Illness as an avenue toward enlightenment. Sometimes, rather than begging for healing, we should pray for insight to better understand this health challenge. Joni Eareckson Tada, was a lovely young lady who was paralyzed in a diving accident, yet found:
Philippians 4:7 *the peace of God, which transcends all understanding*
Her physical crippling led to her spiritual unfolding. Alexander Graham Bell used the deafness of his mother and

wife as inspiration to invent the telephone, by patterning the integral parts of the telephone after a sheep's ear. How many drug and alcohol counselors started off their brilliant and productive careers face down in a gutter? A diamond is nothing more than a piece of coal that was put under extreme pressure for a long period of time.

We now begin this journey of healing together.

CHAPTER 2

◆

THE WISDOM & HEALING POWER OF GOD'S WHOLE FOODS

Exodus15:26 He said, "If you listen carefully to the voice of the LORD your God and do what is right in his eyes, if you pay attention to his commands and keep all his decrees, I will not bring on you any of the diseases I brought on the Egyptians, for I am the LORD, who heals you."

Personal Profile

VM and KM were a busy professional couple with 2 small children. All 4 in the family had a variety of health problems that had not been helped by drugs. VM was constantly on a diet, struggling to lose the 50 pounds she had gained since high school. KM had been on medication for his high blood pressure, which then produced the side effect of impotency. Both for his male ego and their marriage, this was a real problem. One of the children, TM, had been put on medication for her "hyperactive" behavior. The other child, JM, was continuously plagued with colds, sore throats, and tonsillitis.

Since the family's harried lifestyle revolved around fast foods, TV dinners, canned foods, and pizzas delivered; there were numerous nutritional problems to deal with. VM was put on small frequent meals of a low fat diet, rich in fiber from vegetables and whole grains, along with the fat burning supplements of hydroxycitrate (from the fruit Garcinia cambogia), ginseng, chromium polynicotinate, medium chain triglycerides, carnitine, and a broad spectrum supplement. She also began using natural progesterone lotion on her thighs at night to compensate for a common progesterone deficiency. She began an exercise program of 30 minutes daily on her dual action stairclimber, which works both the upper and lower body. Within 6 months, the weight had melted off her and she looked even better than her high school days.

KM was put on a diet rich in fresh fruits, vegetables, beans, and whole grains; with a serious restriction on meats and milk. He was given supplements of broad spectrum vitamins and minerals, plus extra vitamin C, fish oil, magnesium and potassium, and the herb ginkgo biloba. I also sent him to a biofeedback psychologist to help him regulate his blood pressure and a chiropractic physician to help with some chronic back problems. Within 2 months, he no longer needed his blood pressure medication and his potency returned along with considerable extra energy, which won him a handsome bonus and promotion at work.

The children began eating this same healthy diet that the parents were on. TM was given the responsibility of tending the family's fresh vegetable garden in the back yard, and thus had much less time for TV and video games. She suddenly lost the "hyperactive, or attention deficit disorder" label and was put in a class for the gifted students. JM not only ate the nourishing foods that were put on the dinner table, but also took supplements of broad spectrum vitamins and minerals, plus extra beta-carotene, C, E, zinc, a homeopathic remedy for tonsillitis, and the immune stimulating herb echinacea. She was able to cut her sick days away from school by 90%.

---

*N*utrition and health. It makes so much sense: "you are what you eat." Veterinarians know the irreplaceable link between nutrient intake and health. Actually, our pets eat better than most Americans. Your dog or cat probably gets a balanced formula of protein, carbohydrate, fat, fiber, vitamins and minerals. Yet, most of us eat for taste, cost, and convenience.

The most commonly eaten food in America is heavily refined and nutritionally bankrupt white flour. Meanwhile, our livestock eat the more nutritious wheat germ and bran that we discard. When our crops are not doing well, we examine the soil for nutrients, fluid and pH content. Our gardens prosper when we water, fertilize, and add a little broad spectrum mineral supplement.

A sign posted near the junk food vending machines in a major city zoo warns: "Do not feed this food to the animals or they may get sick and die." Think about it. The food that might kill a 400 pound ape is okay for a 40 pound child? If our gardens, field crops, pets, exotic zoo creatures and every other form of life on earth are all heavily dependent on their diet for health, then what makes us think that humans have transcended this God-ordained dependence on nutrition?

There is a basic flaw in our thinking about health care in this country. We treat symptoms, not the underlying cause of the disease. Yet, the only way to provide long-lasting relief in any degenerative disease, like cancer, arthritis and heart disease, is to reverse the basic cause of the disease. For example, let's say that you developed a headache because your neighbor's teenager is playing drums too loudly. You take an aspirin to subdue the headache, then your stomach starts churning. So you take some antacids to ease the stomach nausea, then your blood pressure goes up. And on it goes. We shift symptoms with medication, as if in a bizarre "shell game", when we really need to deal with the fundamental cause of the disease.

Fungus grows on the bark of a tree because of the underlying conditions of heat, moisture and darkness. You could "cut,

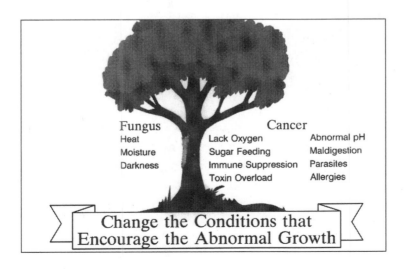

burn, and poison" all you want on this fungus, but the tree will keep making more fungus as long as the underlying conditions are present. Similarly, cancer grows because of the underlying conditions of immune suppression, toxic burden, spiritual depression, malnutrition, hyperglycemia (too much sugar in the blood), hypoxia (too little oxygen), abnormal acid/base balance, hypothyroidism, and more. You can "cut (surgery), burn (radiation), and poison" (chemotherapy) all you want, but the patient keeps making cancer until the underlying conditions have been changed.

Do not get me wrong, medical therapies do reduce tumor burden, but they do not cure cancer. Only your God-given internal healing mechanisms can do that. A full professor of oncology, Dr. Albert Braverman, has been quoted in the prestigious journal, Lancet, claiming that no cancers incurable in 1975 are curable today. Traditional medical therapies have made little progress against cancer because of our "sin", which is translated in Jesus's original Aramaic language as an "error in thinking".

Another example is heart disease. There are over 60,000 miles of blood vessels in the average adult body. When a person develops blockage in the arteries near the heart, open heart bypass surgery will often be recommended. In this procedure, a short section of vein from the leg is used to replace the plugged up vessels near the heart. But what has been done to improve the other 59,999 miles left that are probably equally obstructed? A Harvard professor, Dr. E. Braunwald, investigated the records from thousands of bypass patients in the Veteran's Administration Hospitals and found no improvement in lifespan after this expensive and risky surgery. Why? Because the underlying cause of the disease has not been addressed. Bypass surgery treats the symptoms of heart disease like chemo and radiation treat the symptoms of cancer like drugs temporarily subdue high blood pressure. Each provide temporary relief, but no long term cure, while the underlying problems deteriorates into something much worse.

LEARNING NUTRITION FROM GOD'S WORD

"The doctor of the future will give no medicine, but will involve the patient in the proper use of food, fresh air and exercise." Thomas Edison

Without food processing we wouldn't know much about human nutrition. That's right. When European sailors spent months at sea with an imbalanced diet lacking in fresh fruits and vegetables, they came down with scurvy. Up to half of all trans-oceanic explorers from 1600-1850 died from this common vitamin C deficiency. When we taught the Indonesians how to refine whole grain rice down to white rice, thus removing the valuable thiamin, we discovered beri-beri (literally means "I cannot, I cannot"), which is a thiamin deficiency.

When we decided to remove the fiber from whole fruits, vegetables and grains, we began history's greatest pandemic plague: the diseases of civilization; including obesity, heart disease, cancer, diabetes, gout, arthritis, cataracts, Alzheimer's, and more. When we naively thought that we could duplicate the nutritional value of mother's milk for newborn infants, we later learned of all the minute but critical components in mother's milk; and many thousands of infants died in the learning process.

Everytime we think that we can improve on nature, we find our confidence misplaced. Everytime we fiddle with a wholesome food, we erode its nutrient value. In whole foods lies a universe of nutrients that we will never fully understand but are Divinely placed there for our benefit. Extracting juice from fruits and vegetables makes as much sense as eating white flour or substituting mother's milk with canned cow's milk.

Food is a rich tapestry of thousands of substances. Food contains life-giving agents that we are only beginning to understand. One third of all prescription drugs in America originated as plant products. It is food that provides macronutrients, like carbohydrate, fat and protein, that drive extremely influential hormones and prostaglandins in your body. It is food that establishes your pH balance and electrolyte "soup" that bathes every cell in your body. It is food that contains all the vitamins, minerals, and "sub-nutrients" that have become a hotly researched area. While vitamin and mineral supplements are valuable, they cannot replace the fundamental importance of a wholesome diet.

DIETARY RECOMMENDATIONS

Since the 1964 World Health Organization published their first pamphlet on cancer causes, many prominent health organizations have publicized their own personal version of a "healthy diet". Guidelines on good eating principles have come from the Senate Diet Goals, American Cancer Society, American Dietetic Association, Surgeon General of the United States, United States Public Health Association, American Heart Association, and many more.

While these programs have minor variations, they have much in common. Each of these programs embraces a diet that:

† uses only unprocessed foods, nothing in a package with a label
† uses high amounts of fresh vegetables
† employs a low fat diet
† emphasizes the importance of regularity
† uses low fat dairy or no dairy products, with yogurt as the preferred dairy selection
† stabilizes blood sugar levels with no sweets and never eat something sweet by itself
† increases potassium and reduces sodium intake

More than coincidentally, the diet recommended in Scripture captures the same nutritional guidelines. As you are about to see, God wears many hats, including that of the world's first and greatest nutritionist.

SCRIPTURAL SUPERFOODS

Though there are many nourishing foods, there are only a few superfoods that contain such a potent collection of protective factors that they deserve regular inclusion in most diets. The Bible instructs us on specific foods to include and others to avoid. Thousands of years later and thousands of scientific studies later, these truths stand taller than ever.

† **Low fat.** One of the few areas in which scientists are in near total agreement is that we should eat less fat to improve our health and lifespan. Fat "rusts" in the body as free radicals cause damage to cell membranes and DNA, thus creating heart disease, cancer, and premature aging. Moses could not explain the "why" of these laws to his nomadic people, but we now see an elegant explanation which involves pro-oxidants and biochemistry. More on fat in the A,B,C chapter.

> Leviticus 3:17 *This is a lasting ordinance for the generations to come, wherever you live: You must not eat any fat or any blood.'"*

† **Avoid obesity.** Of all the risk factors that increase the chances for dying young and contracting some major disease, obesity is near the top of the list. Excess calories in the diet are stored as body fat, which is vulnerable to the "rusting" mentioned above, which can clog the arteries, which then starves the organs throughout the body. From the Surgeon General of the United States to the National Academy of Sciences, experts agree on the hazards of obesity. And you first saw such warnings in the Bible.

> Luke 21:34 *And take heed to yourselves, lest at any time your hearts be overcharged with surfeiting [overeating], and drunkenness, and cares of this life, and so that day come upon you unawares.*

† **Plant food.** Fruits, vegetables, whole grains, legumes, seeds, and nuts are a rich stew of nutrients. According to a professor of nutrition at the University of California at Berkeley, and published in the Journal of the National Cancer Institute,

there are over 200 peer-reviewed journal articles showing that a diet rich in fruits and vegetables will dramatically lower the risk for cancer and heart disease.

> Genesis1:29 *Then God said, "I give you every seed-bearing plant on the face of the whole earth and every tree that has fruit with seed in it. They will be yours for food.*

While we have only scratched the surface in understanding the nutritional value of God's plant food, unprocessed plant food contains:

> † over 20,000 different bioflavonoids, now highly regarded as anti-oxidants to slow the disease process with the ability to chelate heavy metals out of the body
> † over 800 different carotenoids to stimulate immune function and slow aging
> † phytochemicals beyond belief, like genistein in soy and indoles in cabbage which have impressed the National Cancer Institute with anti-cancer properties
> † abundant potassium for regulating cell functions
> † and an endless array of health-giving substances.

Some of the nutrients in plant food cannot even be digested, like fiber. And it was our arrogance and ignorance that allowed 20th century food manufacturers to remove fiber from our food supply, only to result in millions of unnecessary and premature deaths.

Hipppocrates, father of modern medicine 2400 years ago, first noticed that whole grain bread provided roughage to bulk the stools. Sylvester Graham preached the message of finely ground whole wheat flour to "cure what ails you" back in the early 19th century, thus inventing the "Graham" cracker. Dr. John Harvey Kellogg founded his healing sanitorium and a cereal empire in Battle Creek, Michigan in the later 19th century with such a simple principle as adding fiber back to the diet to cure a myriad of conditions.

Generations later, Dr. Dennis Burkitt, a medical missionary from England to Africa, first proposed in 1970 that this "useless" fiber which we remove from our modern food was actually quite essential to detoxify the body and prevent many illnesses. We can now scientifically link obesity, heart disease, appendicitis, cancer, gout, arthritis, hemorrhoids, diverticulitis, and other common conditions to the stripping of fiber from our food supply.

God put fiber in the food supply for a reason. There are other life-giving phytochemicals that we are unintentionally removing in the processing of plants. Everytime we think that we know more than God, we pay the consequences. After the Garden of Eden (Genesis 3:23) and Tower of Babel (Genesis 11:9) debacles, you'd think that we would have learned this lesson by now.

† **Clean Meat.** Before the flood, God's people were vegetarians. Yet, after the flood, God gave us permission to eat meat, but provided strict guidelines on what meat was acceptable.

> Leviticus11:2-3 *'Of all the animals that live on land, these are the ones you may eat: You may eat any animal that has a split hoof completely divided and that chews the cud.*

We now know that toxins accumulate as you move up the food chain. In other words, meat-eating creatures have more poisons in them than vegetarian creatures. The Book of Leviticus is written by Moses as his people are about to enter the promised land of Canaan, where the Canaanites eat just about anything. God told His people to eat vegetarian animals that thoroughly chew their food and have multi-chambered stomachs. Today, as a professional nutritionist, I can fully appreciate these laws, since these animals are more likely to be free from disease, infections, and parasites.

Cows, sheep, chicken, and turkey were allowed under God's decree. While modern nutritionists sometimes criticize the consumption of beef, cows in Moses' day were range fed, lower in fat, and not grown on chemicals. Cows are okay. Our polluted and high fat cows of today are not okay. Pigs do not chew their cud and eat just about anything, which makes them more likely to carry infections in their meat, including trichinosis, a tiny worm. Sheep are rich in omega-3 fats, which are shown to be very healthy. And scientists now encourage the regular consumption of chicken and turkey, due to their high protein and low fat content.

We are then told to eat certain fish with fins and scales. Creatures of the sea with shells, like shrimp and lobster and clams, are filter feeders and are more likely to gather poisons since they do not swim the seas. Clean fish would include salmon, haddock, halibut, sole, tuna, and sea bass. Nutritionally speaking, these foods are rich in a variety of nutrients which improve circulation and immune function. Scientists find that just 2 servings of fish each week cut heart disease risk by 40%!

Leviticus 11:9 *Of all the creatures living in the water of the seas and the streams, you may eat any that have fins and scales.*

We are then told throughout Leviticus 11 that we should not eat camel, rabbit, hawk, raven, owl, and other creatures which are "unclean". Animals that eat other animals (carnivores) concentrate poisons in their flesh. Scavengers eat dead meat which is loaded with bacteria and parasites, which can be neutralized and tolerated by the scavenger, but not by the person who eats the scavenger. Scientists today find that the few remaining cannibals around the world oftentimes suffer from a rare virus disease in the brain, which comes from eating other carnivores (man).

† Garlic.

Numbers 11:5 *We remember the fish we ate in Egypt at no cost--also the cucumbers, melons, leeks, onions and garlic.*

This stinky little vegetable has been used for 5000 years in various healing formulas. In many studies, garlic has been found to lower blood pressure, lower cholesterol in the blood, cleanse the blood of impurities, increase vigor, jump start the immune system, prevent cancer, and more. Garlic is used with such frequency in Chinese medicine that it is sometimes referred to as "Chinese penicillin".

Pasteur noted that garlic killed all of the bacteria in his petri dishes. Garlic has been found to stimulate natural protection against tumor cells. Tarig Abdullah, MD of Florida found that white blood cells from garlic-fed people were able to kill 139% more tumor cells than white cells from non-garlic eaters. Garlic and onions fed to lab animals helped to decrease the number of skin tumors. Researchers found that onions provided major protection against expected tumors from DMBA in test animals. Mice with a genetic weakness toward cancer were fed raw garlic with a lower-than-expected tumor incidence.

The most common form of cancer worldwide is stomach cancer. Chinese researchers find that a high intake of garlic and onions cuts the risk for stomach cancer in half. Garlic provides the liver with a certain amount of protection against carcinogenic chemicals. Scientists find that garlic is deadly to invading pathogens or tumor cells, but is harmless to normal healthy body cells; thus offering the hope of the truly selective toxin against cancer that is being sought worldwide.

† Carotenoids.

> Genesis 1:30 *And to all the beasts of the earth and all the birds of the air and all the creatures that move on the ground--everything that has the breath of life in it—I give every green plant for food." And it was so.*

Green plants create sugars by capturing the sun's energy in a process called photosynthesis. The electrons that must be corralled in this process can be highly destructive. Hence, God has created an impressive system of free radical protectors, including carotenoids and bioflavonoids, that act like the lead lining in a nuclear reactor to absorb dangerous unpaired electrons.

Both of these substances have potential in stimulating the immune system and slowing down the aging process.

Carotenoids are found in green and orange fruits and vegetables. Bioflavonoids are found in citrus, whole grains, honey, and other plant foods.

† **Cruciferous vegetables.** Broccoli, brussel sprouts, cabbage, and cauliflower were involved in the "ground floor" discovery of phytochemicals in plants. Lee Wattenberg, PhD of the University of Minnesota found in the 1970s that animals fed cruciferous vegetables had markedly lower cancer rates than matched controls. Since then, the active ingredient "indoles" have been isolated from cruciferous vegetables and found to be very protective against cancer. Scientists at Johns Hopkins University found that lab animals fed cruciferous vegetables and then exposed to the deadly carcinogen aflatoxin had a 90 percent reduction in their cancer rate. Cruciferous vegetables are able to increase the body's production of glutathione peroxidase, which is one of the more important protective enzyme systems in the body. Cruciferous vegetables help to bind up estrogen in the body to lower the risk for breast and ovarian cancers.

† **Barley.**

Deuteronomy 8:8 ...*a land with wheat and barley, vines and fig trees, pomegranates, olive oil and honey*

While America is obsessed with wheat as our principle grain, barley is actually a healthier grain. Jesus ate barley bread at Passover, in his miracle of feeding the multitudes, and at the Last Supper. Barley is rich in tocotrienols, a substance that may be more potent than vitamin E at slowing the disease and aging process. Barley is less likely to cause allergic reactions, such as are common with wheat. Barley plants are more drought and insect resistant than wheat. Countries that favor barley as their primary grain have a much lower incidence of heart disease than America. Right now, barley is a second-class grain in America, used primarily for making beer and other alcohol.

† Apple.

Song of Solomon 2:5 *Strengthen me with raisins, refresh me with apples, for I am faint with love.*

Apples are a wonder. Rich in the soluble fiber, pectin, apples can help cleanse the colon, while lowering the amount of cholesterol in the blood. Apples also are a cleansing food for the teeth, almost as effective as brushing or flossing the teeth. Apples last a long time in a climate-controlled root cellar. Apples make fine cider vinegar, which is loaded with its own healing properties.

† Fish.

Mark 6:41 *Taking the five loaves and the two fish and looking up to heaven, he gave thanks and broke the loaves.*

Fish are a rich source of protein and are usually low in fat, while containing a fat that has major therapeutic abilities. Scientists began wondering why Eskimos, who eat 60% of the their calories from fat, and have virtually no vitamin C, fiber, or vegetables in their diet somehow have very little cancer or heart disease. The answer to this riddle came in the 1970s as the special fat, EPA, was discovered in fish and has enormous healing properties. EPA can reduce the inflammation of arthritis, bolster immune functions, thin the blood to prevent strokes, feed the brain a crucial fat for nerve function, help dilate blood vessels for better circulation, and even lower fats in the blood.

Fish are also rich in vitamin B-6 and the mineral selenium, which are in short supply in the American diet. Without fish in the diet, many societies end up with epidemic levels of goiter, a serious deficiency of the mineral iodine. The World Bank tells us that over 1 billion people the world over are physically and mentally handicapped because of low iodine diets.

Jesus gathered His disciples from fishermen. He used many parables regarding fish. He fed the multitudes with fish and during the Roman persecution of Christians, Christ was symbolized by the fish sign, now used to represent one's dedication to Christ. Fish are very special in the Bible and incredibly useful to your body.

† Honey.

Genesis 43:11 Put some of the best products of the land in your bags and take them down to the man as a gift--a little balm and a little honey, some spices and myrrh, some pistachio nuts and almonds.

Humans are born with an affinity for sweet things, like mother's milk. Honey and fruit are among the sweet foods that can actually be good for us. Honey, on the surface, is just another simple carbohydrate, like refined white sugar. But a more detailed analysis shows us that honey is high in fructose, which is healthier than the sucrose and glucose found in white sugar. Honey also contains some chromium, a mineral required to help the body process sugars. Honey is a good source of bioflavonoids, which help to slow the aging process and fight infections. Honey has amazing antibiotic properties, and has been used topically to help prevent infections in cuts. Honey is a pre-digested food that bees gather from flower pollen.

Remember the old expression from the marvelous play/movie Mary Poppins, "a spoonful of sugar (honey?) helps the medicine go down". We can add modest amounts of honey to tea, cereal, breads, and elsewhere to make the food even tastier. Used in moderation, honey can help to make otherwise bland but nourishing food more palatable.

> Proverbs 25:16 *If you find honey, eat just enough--too much of it, and you will vomit.*

† **Legumes.** Beans are amazing. Whereas many crops drain the soil of nutrient content, beans actually add fertility (nitrogen) to the soil while they are growing. Beans are incredibly rich in protein and could go a long way toward solving the world's famine problems. Notice how many people can be fed from an acre of soybeans versus an acre of raising cattle.

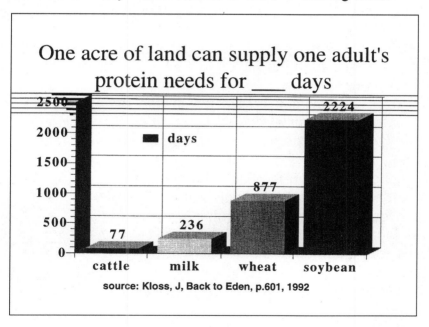

One acre of land can supply one adult's protein needs for ___ days

- days

cattle	77
milk	236
wheat	877
soybean	2224

source: Kloss, J, Back to Eden, p.601, 1992

Beans will last a long time in dry cool storage. In the highly publicized studies showing that oat fiber could lower serum cholesterol, the press forgot to mention that the same benefits were shown in bean fiber. Soybeans are a virtual cornucopia of useful products, from lecithin (good for the arteries and nerves), to soy milk (good for people with dairy allergies), to soy protein (cheap and very concentrated), to the genistein in soy which helps to fight cancer.

Legumes have a substance that can partially protect the seed from digestion, called protease inhibitors (PI). For many years, these substances were thought to be harmful. New evidence finds that PIs may squelch tumor growth. Researchers at the National Cancer Institute find a collection of substances in soybeans, including isoflavones and phytoestrogens, appear to have potent anti-cancer properties. Dr. Ann Kennedy has spent 20 years researching a compound in soybeans that prevents and even slows down cancer in most animals exposed to a variety of carcinogens, lowers the toxic side effects of chemo and radiation therapy, and even reverts a cancer cell back to a normal healthy cell.

For a real treat, try some delicious high protein Ezekial bread that was specified in the Bible. Make it yourself, or buy it in the grocery store.

> Ezekial 4:9 *Take wheat and barley, beans and lentils, millet and spelt; put them in a storage jar and use them to make bread for yourself.*

Though people in the Old Testament did not know it, their Ezekial bread employed "complimentary proteins", meaning that combining grains with legumes at the same meal, yields a protein of similar quality to that of steak.

† Yogurt.

> Isaiah 7:15, 22 *He will eat curds and honey when he knows enough to reject the wrong and choose the right.*

"Curd", or curdled milk, appears to be nothing more than a

fermented dairy product. Yet, modern scientists find that the active culture of bacteria in yogurt (Lactobacillus) can fortify the immune system. In both humans and animals, yogurt in the diet tripled the internal production of interferon, a powerful weapon of the immune system against tumor cells, while also raising the level of natural killer cells. Yogurt has been shown to slow down the growth of tumor cells in the GI tract while improving the ability of the immune system to destroy active tumor cells. Yogurt can block the production of carcinogenic agents in the colon.

When scientists looked at the diet of 1010 women with breast cancer and compared them to an equally matched group without breast cancer, they found that the more yogurt consumed, the lower the risk for breast cancer.

In several European studies, yogurt in animal studies was able to reverse tumor progress. A 1962 study found that 59 percent of 258 mice implanted with sarcoma cells were cured through yogurt. A more recent American study found a 30 percent cure rate in animals through yogurt.

Yogurt also lowers fats in the blood, for a reduced heart disease risk. Yogurt improves both constipation and diarrhea. Yogurt taken internally and as a douche helps many women with their vaginal yeast infections. Yogurt improves the general health of the gastro-intestinal tract, which is where many experts feel the aging process begins.

† **Others.** There are numerous foods that have amazing healing properties, including apricots, citrus fruit, cranberries, fiber, figs, ginger, green tea, pomegranates, spinach, and seaweed. All the more reason to encourage a mixed highly nutritious diet for optimal health and vigor. More on these other healthy foods from God's kitchen in chapter 5.

SYNERGISTIC FORCES IN WHOLE FOODS

Although 1000 mg daily of vitamin C has been shown to reduce the risk for stomach cancer, a small glass of orange juice containing only 37 mg of vitamin C is twice as likely to lower the chances for stomach cancer. Something in whole oranges is even more chemo-protective than vitamin C. Although most people only absorb 20-50% of their ingested calcium, the remaining calcium binds up potentially damaging fats in the intestines to provide protection against colon cancer.

In 1963, a major "player" in the American drug business, Merck, tried to patent a single antibiotic substance that was originally isolated from yogurt. But this substance did not work alone. Since then, researchers have found no less than 7 natural antibiotics that all contribute to yogurt's unique ability to protect the body from infections. There are many healing agents in food, including chlorophyll, over 800 different carotenoids (including beta-carotene), over 20,000 different bioflavonoids (including rutin and pycnogenol), lycopenes (in tomatoes), genistein (in soybeans) and thousands more.

In a "good", "better", and "best" approach to rating nutrition efforts; "good" is juicing fruits and vegetables, "better" is pureeing to maintain all the wholesome value of the fruit and vegetable, and "best" is to eat the whole fruit and vegetable. The point is: we can isolate and concentrate certain factors in foods for use as therapeutic supplements, such as taking a pill of vitamin C, but we must always rely heavily on the Divine and mysteriously elegant symphony of ingredients found in whole food for vigorous health.

DWELL ON THESE THOUGHTS
EACH NIGHT BEFORE GOING TO SLEEP

Psalms 103:2 *Praise the Lord, O my soul, and forget not all His benefits, Who forgives all your sins and heals all your diseases.*

Jeremiah 17:14 *Heal me, O LORD, and I will be healed; save me and I will be saved, for you are the one I praise.*

Psalms 23:4 *Even though I walk through the valley of the shadow of death, I will fear no evil, for you are with me; your rod and your staff, they comfort me.*

2Corinthians 3:4 *Such confidence as this is ours through Christ before God.*

Psalms 119:28 *My soul is weary with sorrow; strengthen me according to your word.*

Philippians 4:13 *I can do everything through him who gives me strength.*

CHAPTER 3

$\blacklozenge$

THE A, B, Cs
OF HEALING

1Corinthians 10:31 *Whether you eat or drink or whatever you do,. do it all for the glory of God.*

Personal Profile

AJ was a busy in-demand minister with a huge congregation—and his health was failing. He was overweight, lacked energy, had been through quadruple bypass surgery 3 years ago, took medication for his high cholesterol, and was regularly popping nitroglycerin to ease the sharp angina pain in his chest.

I put him on a program that is found throughout this book, including a diet of low fat unprocessed (read: God's) foods, lots of garlic, 30 minutes on the cross country skiing device each morning while he watched his Cable News Network update, supplements of broad spectrum vitamins and minerals, plus extra vitamin C, E, Coenzyme Q-10, fish oil, magnesium, carnitine, and the heart strengthening herb Hawthorne. He went back to the ritual of 30 minutes of quiet meditation each night before going to bed, a habit that he had given up when his ministry became so hectic. Within 3 months, his congregation began asking him what he was doing that made his look so much healthier and younger. Within 6 months, he was off medication and had no more problems with angina pain. His angiogram showed a marked reduction in the blockage of his arteries. He was a new man and was pleasantly surprised when I showed him that many of my health prescriptions came straight out of the Bible!

SIMPLE BIBLICAL SOLUTIONS
FOR COMPLEX MODERN HEALTH PROBLEMS.

ost medical therapies have been serious disappointments in treating degenerative diseases, including heart disease, cancer, stroke, arthritis, diabetes, osteoporosis, Alzheimer's disease and more. After decades of work from brilliant scientists, there is always another unexpected obstacle around the bend that leads to toxic side effects and reduced therapeutic value.

The reason for these frustrating results is our arrogance. Technology has brought us trips to the moon, powerful notebook computers, laser surgery and satellite communications. But in spite of our accomplishments, we cannot make a baby, or an apple, or even a feather. Life is far more complex than many people are willing to admit.

I have had fascinating discussions with many brilliant medical researchers, who, in their brilliance, ignore the laws of nature. Since we cannot veto these biochemical laws of how we function, we need to better understand and work with them. It is unlikely that we will ever develop a "magic bullet" against any degenerative disease. Using some medicine to counteract the destructive influence of the typical American diet is as futile as trying to sweep back the ocean. The simple answers to the complex health puzzle will involve nourishing the God-ordained life forces while eliminating physical and spiritual poisons from the body.

Read the following list over and over until these concepts steep in your subconscious.

Antioxidants slow aging and prevent disease. Life is a continuous balancing act between free radicals (fires) and antioxidants (fire extinguishers). We want to fully oxygenate the tissue, which generates free radicals, but we also want to protect healthy tissue from excess oxidative destruction, using  anti-oxidants. Fresh whole fruits and vegetables are loaded with well studied anti-oxidants (like beta-carotene and vitamin C) and newly discovered anti-oxidants (like bioflavonoids). Anti-oxidants include beta-carotene, C, E, selenium, zinc, riboflavin, manganese, cysteine, methionine, N-acetylcysteine, and many herbal extracts (i.e. green tea, pycnogenols, curcumin).

WHAT TO DO: Go for the color. The rich color of sweet potatoes has more anti-oxidants than white potatoes. Same for red grapes vs. white, dark green leafy vegetables (like collards and spinach) vs iceberg lettuce. Take anti-oxidants as supplements: about 1000 mg of vitamin C, 25,000 iu of beta-carotene, 400 iu of vitamin E, 200 mcg of selenium, and perhaps others.

B

Back maintenance. The nervous system is at the core of our bodily functions. The spinal cord is the extension of the brain, providing us with muscular movement and organ functions. The spine can have alignment problems, due to poor posture, the constant pull of gravity, aging, accidents and falls, atrophied muscles, and obesity. We need to keep the back strong, supple, and properly aligned; which then allows the spinal column to properly direct the functions in our organs, skin, and muscles.

WHAT TO DO: Develop muscles in your neck and back region through regular exercise. One of the best exercises is simply to hold on to a bar that is soundly anchored above your head and let your body weight hang. This procedure will help the spinal vertebra to stretch out and avoid crimping nerves that radiate from the spinal region. Wear shoes with good support in the arches. Choose your bed and chairs with care, since furniture helps to shape the back. Maintain good posture while sitting. For a few minutes at the end of each day, lay on the floor with your lower legs (calf) resting up on a footstool. This position helps your lower back. See your chiropractic physician at least once each year, and more if needed.

Chew your food to a liquid before swallowing. Digestion begins in the mouth with the mechanical mashing of food and the addition of enzymes from saliva. When food is swallowed too quickly, problems result: 1) the food will not be thoroughly digested, which means it cannot be absorbed into the body, 2) we dramatically increase the possibility of overeating, since it requires about 20 minutes for food in the stomach to register to the appetite center of the brain. 3) large chunks of food in the gut tend to putrefy and ferment, giving gas and stimulating the growth of unhealthy bacteria.

WHAT TO DO: Chew your food until it is nearly a liquid or paste; that may mean 20 to 50 bites per mouthful, depending on the food. Use minimal amounts of fluids while you are eating your meal. Fluids dilute digestive juices and make digestion less efficient. Drink your fluids between meals.

Decisions and consequences. Thousands of times every day, we make decisions that affect today and tomorrow. Some people think: "I'll just eat all that unhealthy food in the freezer, then I will start my diet." Rarely works, and only serves to fuel a feeding frenzy. Some say: "I'll eat, but I won't enjoy that low calorie food until I can get my weight under control, then I'll go back to my old eating habits." These people end up practicing the "rhythm method of girth control" as their weight goes up and down, with the net effect being a deterioration in overall health.

Jesus taught us with many parables about planting seeds. Every thought, word, and deed is a prayer; and is planting a "seed" to be harvested soon or eventually. A harsh word to your mate is planting a seed of a weed that can choke off good relations. A binge eating session is planting a seed that will mature into a problem. We can plant alfalfa sprout seeds in our kitchen sprout garden which will be harvested and enjoyed in only a week. We plant other seeds, such as tomato and squash in our summer vegetable garden, which is harvested within a few months. We plant other seeds, like the Biblical mustard seeds, and enjoy a beautiful shade tree decades later. We can even plant redwood seeds and someone else will enjoy the harvest centuries later, such as Jesus did in founding the Christian faith. Know that "as you sow, you reap". Make sure that you are sowing seeds of good health and vitality to enjoy later on.

All lifestyle factors are health vectors. Vectors are forces, which vary in strength and direction. For instance, a small plane flying at 100 miles per hour north into a head wind at 120 mph has a ground speed of -20 mph. Progress is seriously impaired by the opposing force of the wind.

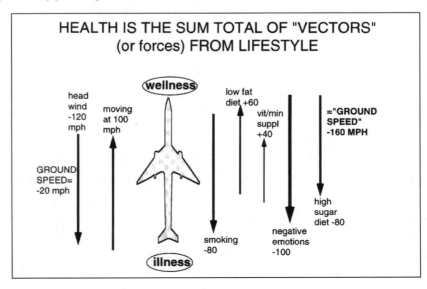

**HEALTH IS THE SUM TOTAL OF "VECTORS"
(or forces) FROM LIFESTYLE**

head wind -120 mph

moving at 100 mph

wellness

low fat diet +60

vit/min suppl +40

="GROUND SPEED" -160 MPH

GROUND SPEED= -20 mph

smoking -80

negative emotions -100

high sugar diet -80

illness

All lifestyle factors are vectors which either move you toward illness or wellness. Consider the person who is smoking (-80 mph), eats a low fat diet (+60 mph), takes vitamin supplements (+40 mph), has a stressful attitude (-100 mph), and eats a high sugar diet (-80). The overwhelming direction for this person is toward illness, even though he or she is doing some things right. Health is a sum total of vectors. For optimal health, get all vectors heading in a favorable direction.

The more wellness you have, the less illness you can have. Just like darkness is the absence of light, disease is the absence of wellness. Curing illness is a matter of replacing it with wellness. The same unhealthy lifestyle may create heart disease in 30% of the people, cancer in 25%, arthritis in 10%, and mental illness in 5%. In a very important step toward removing illness, simply allow wellness to infiltrate the body and mind.

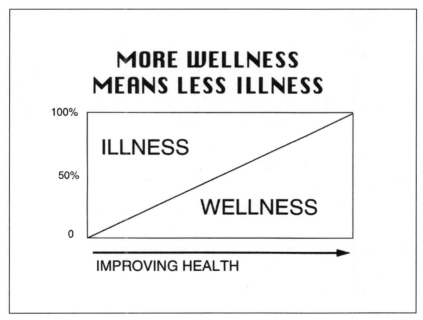

We all operate on two simple motivating factors: seek pleasure and avoid discomfort. If we start a program that we feel will take away our pleasure and give us discomfort, then this program is doomed to failure. In order to permanently change your lifestyle, you will have to prove to yourself that it will be pleasurable in the long run. The new foods that you will be eating can be made tasty and will require a 21 day adaptation period for taste bud adjustment. Think of the extra energy you will have through this new health program, of being sick less often, of living a longer life, of your new found figure and confidence, of being able to enjoy weekends and holidays doing something active rather than glued to the couch.

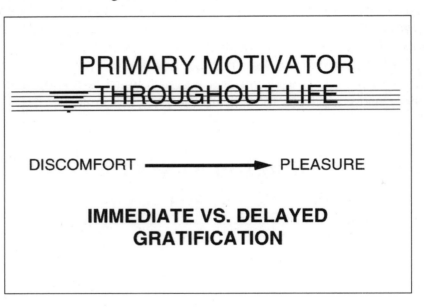

WHAT TO DO: Invest time, money, and effort in your health. Make time for wellness or you will be forced to make time for illness. Think of the advantages of your wellness program. Make it fun and enjoyable or you will not continue. Consider this a lifetime program, not a temporary "diet".

Ethnic background. Pay homage to your native ancestral diet. If you want to appreciate the diversity of life on earth, then stroll through a big city zoo . There are creatures that eat mostly meat, like cats, who would die on a vegetarian diet. There are creatures, like elephants and rabbits, that are strict vegetarians and would die on a carnivorous diet. There are many shades of gray in between these two extremes, like omnivorous humans. The five billion people on the planet earth comprise an incredible tapestry of biochemical and physical diversity. Eskimos eat a diet primarily composed of high fat fish, with almost no fruit, vegetables, or fiber; yet they are an incredibly hardy group of people, nearly devoid of heart disease, cancer or diabetes. They are eating their "God-given factory specification" diet to which they have adapted. Some groups of people have evolved to depend entirely on their dairy herds, while other groups are vegetarians.

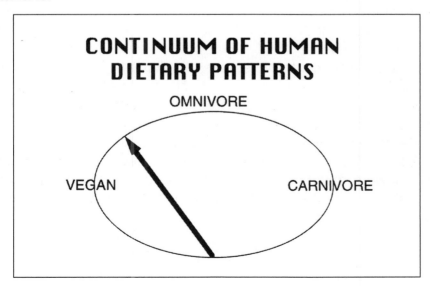

WHAT TO DO: Our ancestors of Abraham's era (roughly 5000 years ago) were mostly hunters and gathers. In colder climates, such as northern Europe, plant food was only available throughout the summer and fall. Lean wild game, fish, stored grains and nuts provided the bulk of food intake throughout winter with summer bringing the fresh produce of vegetables and fruit. In warmer climates, like central Africa and India, the inhabitants relied on a year-round diet of mostly fresh plant food with less meat. Only a few ethnic groups can thrive on dairy products after weaning—for most people a diet rich in dairy products is a bad idea. There are many dietary needs in between these extremes. The take home lesson here is: "eat what you are supposed to eat from your ancient heritage." The more mixed your ethnic background, the less important this issue becomes.

Fat control; both in the body and diet. A high fat diet brings many hazards:

1. a concentrated calorie source, which few sedentary Americans need

2. a more concentrated source of pollutants, since many toxins are fat soluble and are stored in plant and animal fat

3. dietary fat is very likely to end up as body fat, which then begins its slow "rusting" process of free radical activity, which accelerates the disease and aging process

A lot of fat in the body clogs the arteries and burdens the heart, lowers metabolism, squeezes the gut and lungs, is likely to "rust" and generate cancer-causing free radicals, and generally creates havoc in the body.

WHAT TO DO:
TO REDUCE FAT IN THE BODY: SAFE, NATURAL AND PERMANENT WEIGHT REDUCTION

NUTRITION: Eat and enjoy your food. Do not skip meals. Concentrate on foods high in fiber and fluid (vegetables, fruit, grains, legumes, water). Minimize pastries, alcohol, high sugar, and fat foods. Calories do count! To avoid overeating, have soups and salads 20 minutes before mealtime and drink a glass of water just before the meal. Eat until satisfied, not stuffed. Do not consume less than 800 calories per day without medical supervision.

EXERCISE: This is essential to successful weight control. Must be fun, vigorous, and regular (minimum 3 times/week at 1 hour each session). Strive for improvement in strength, flexibility, and cardiovascular fitness. Start gradually with non-stress bearing routines like biking, swimming, and fast walking. Join supportive exercise groups.

BEHAVIOR MODIFICATION: Eat and chew slowly. Put your fork down between each bite. Allow at least 20 minutes for each meal. Use small plates. Keep leftovers out of sight. Keep snack foods out of your house. Leave a bite on each plate to signal satiety. Put leftovers in refrigerator, not in your mouth. Know the environmental cues (e.g. TV, reading, driving) which make you eat. Avoid these cues or substitute other behaviors like crafts. Eat only at the table at mealtime. Pre-plan meals. Do not shop for food when hungry. Enjoy your meals with candles, music, nice clothes, etc. Store food in opaque containers. Plan soups and casseroles for leftovers. Keep a written record of what & how much you eat & mood at that time.

ATTITUDE: Never say "diet". This is a lifetime program of healthy living. Set realistic goals and reward yourself (not with food) when you reach these goals. Deal with the moods (e.g. depression, boredom, self-pity) which provoke an appetite. Talk to friends, or seek professional counseling. Accept total responsibility for your life and weight. Seek the support of friends and family. No one can sabotage your efforts if you don't want them to. If you expect someone or something else to do it for you, or a "cure" for overweight, or immediate results; then you will likely fail at losing. Be prepared for thinness, you will be healthier and happier, but life will not be perfect. See yourself as thin. Eat and exercise accordingly. Know the difference between biological hunger and psychological appetite. Subdue the latter. Do not be discouraged or torture yourself after an occasional binge. Reaffirm your desire to be lithe & healthy. Join support groups. Eat your planned food before going to parties & avoid high calorie appetizers OR exercise extra and eat less BEFORE the party to allow for slight overindulgence. You, too, can be lean, attractive, healthy, energetic & long lived.

"Pinch an inch" means that skinfold thickness is a good indicator of your total body fat. Other, more accurate devices that help to plot your progress toward leanness include a combination weight scale with bio-impedance (Tanita Corp., 708-581-0250) or infra-red scanner (Futrex 800-545-1950). These devices tell you how much of your body is fat, thus giving you a "quality" of weight reading rather than the usual bathroom scale, which only tells you "quantity" of weight.

TO REDUCE FAT IN THE DIET:

Follow the chart below and eat more low fat foods. This one principle alone will make a huge difference in your waistline and health. Best oils to use in the kitchen: olive, which is referred to often in the Bible. Butter is better than margarine, since butter is God's food and margarine is a synthetic derivative of hydrogenated oils. Borage, flax, and primrose oils can be valuable therapeutic supplements. Take a tablespoon each day of emulsified flavored cod liver oil or flax oil. Medium chain triglycerides (MCT) are processed in the body more like a carbohydrate than a fat, and can assist in weight loss. MCT oils are available through Allergy (800-USE-FLAX) or Sound Nutrition (800-43-SOUND) and can be used in the kitchen, along with olive and canola oils.

% FAT CALORIES IN FOODS

>75%	50-75	40-50	30-40	20-30	<20%
avocado, bacon, beef, coconut, cold cuts, cream, cheese, nuts, olives, peanut butter, sausage, seeds	beef rump, pound cake, canadian bacon, cheddar & swiss cheese, chicken w. skin, chocolate candy, cream soups, eggs, ice cream, trout, oysters, ham, tuna	lean hamburger or T-bone, fried chicken, mackerel, whole milk, pumpkin pie, canned salmon, turkey pot pie	chuck steak, roast chicken w/o skin, haddock, halibut, granola, 2% milk, pizza, roast turkey, low fat yogurt	lean sirloin, corn muffin, cod, liver, pancakes, tomato soup, wheat germ	beans, peas, lentil, buttermilk, angel food cake, most cereals, perch, fruit, whole grains, skim milk, tuna in water, vegetables, roast white turkey

➞ **BEST**

CUTTING THE FAT: chose to lose

Instead of:	kcal	chose:	kcal
doughnut	235	plain muffin	120
peanuts 1/2 c	420	popcorn, 2 c plain	108
fried chicken, 3 oz dark w.skin	240	roast chicken, 3 oz white w/o skin	145
ice cream 1/2 c	135	low fat yogurt	75
rib roast 4 oz	300	lean flank steak	200
whole milk 1 c	150	skim milk	85
choc. cake w. icing	310	angel food cake	121

God's food is better than man's food. God had something wonderful in mind when He created our nutrient-rich food supply. Don't settle for anything less.

WHAT TO DO: Shop the perimeter of the grocery store. On the outside aisles you will find fresh fruit and vegetables, fish, poultry, dairy, eggs, and bread—God's food, straight up. Grow your own food, if possible, like a vegetable garden or sprouts in the kitchen year round. Buy organic produce and range-fed poultry and meat, if possible. If your food will not rot or sprout then throw it out. God's food is full of life and therefore has a shelf life. Food processors are more interested in longer shelf life than longer human life. If you can't figure out where the food came from in God's kingdom, then put it back on the grocery store shelf. Ever seen Spam running wild through the woods? Ever raised a Twinkie in your garden or picked an Oreo in an orchard?

Help yourself to whole grains, vegetables, legumes, fruit, lean fish and poultry. These are the staples of a good diet. It is difficult to get overweight on these high fiber and low fat foods.

WHAT TO DO: Eat lots of fresh vegetables, some of which should be uncooked, especially green and orange fruits and vegetables, like carrots and collards. Add a generous portion of

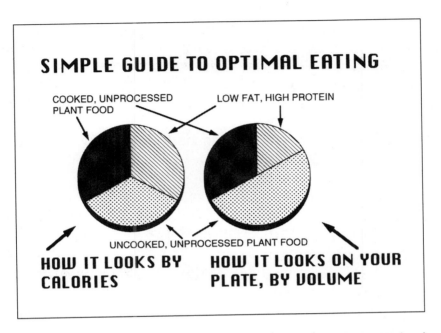

whole grains and legumes, which need to be either cooked or sprouted to be digestible. Add smaller amounts of raw fruit, fish, poultry, sheep, lean beef, nuts, and seeds. Add a cup of yogurt each day, if you can tolerate dairy products.

Immune system—bolstering the body's defense mechanisms. We have an extensive network of protective factors that circulate throughout our bodies to kill any bacteria, virus, yeast or cancer cells. Think of these 20 trillion immune cells as both your Department of Defense and your waste disposal company. It is the surveillance of an alert and capable immune system that defends most of us from infections, allergies, auto-immune dis eases, cancer, and premature aging. A healthy immune soldier will either eat its prey (phagocytosis) or splash toxic free radicals on it (chemotaxis). Either way, if the immune soldier is well protected with anti-oxidants (see the letter A), then your immune system will have better recognition of invaders and a higher kill rate.

WHAT TO DO: Avoid substances that will shut down the immune system; including:

- † toxic metals, like lead, cadmium and mercury
- † volatile organic chemicals, from agriculture and industry
- † sugar
- † omega-6 fats, like soy and corn oil
- † stress and worry, and more.

Include substances that can enhance the immune system:

- † vitamins, like A, beta-carotene, C, E, and B-6
- † quasi-vitamins, like Coenzyme Q-10; EPA, ALA, and GLA (special fats)
- † minerals, like zinc, chromium, and selenium
- † amino acids, like arginine and glutathione
- † herbal extracts, like echinecea, ginseng, Pau D'arco, and astragalus
- † nutrient factors, like yogurt, garlic, cabbage, enzymes and fresh green leafy vegetables.
- † positive emotions, like love, forgiveness and creative visualization

Jesus as our role model. For many reasons, Jesus was our Savior. Jesus showed us how to live, love, laugh, and forgive. He healed the sick, raised the dead, and in the end conquered death and sin for all of us. Jesus ate God's nourishing food and exercised Himself into a lean fit figure. Jesus fed the crowd of 5000 using only 2 fish and 5 loaves of barley. Fish and barley bread is a meal that I can readily endorse as a nutritionist.

Jesus also taught us to give thanks for what we have and you will get more. Jesus did not worry that his meager basket of food would not feed the multitudes. We can learn much from this Scriptural passagae. Not only should we give thanks for our healthy God-given food before eating, but we should also give thanks for what works on our body. Instead of complaining about the aches and pains, think about what works. If you are alive, then something on your body is working. Dwell on and give thanks for your good health and you will get more of it.

Matthew 13:12 *Whoever has will be given more, and he will have an abundance. Whoever does not have, even what he has will be taken from him.*

KISS method of "Keep It Simple, Student". If I had to reduce all of the studies on nutrition and health maintenance into a short paragraph, then here it is. Photocopy this list and tape it to your refrigerator.

Dr. Quillin's Ultimate Health Tips
1. Eat God's food, not mankind's. Shop the perimeter of the grocery store.
2. Maintain a healthy gut through fiber, fluid, and yogurt or probiotics. Chew food to a liquid before swallowing. Drink minimal fluids with meal.
3. Take appropriate nutritional supplements in addition to, rather

than instead of, good eating habits.

4. Minimize fat, sweets, salt, and alcohol.

5. Exercise & eat to leanness—an inch of skinfold thickness at hip bone.

6. Drink lots of clean water.

7. Emphasize vegetables, whole grains, legumes, lean fish & poultry, and fruit; with nuts and seeds in smaller amounts.

8. Tolerance: 90% of food intake should be nourishing, 10% can be "others". This allows us an occasional indulgence in non-nourishing foods.

9. Detoxify; stop taking in toxins and get rid of what you have in your body.

10. Live, love, laugh, learn, forgive, sing praises, and seek peace. Give thanks and focus on what you have spiritually, emotionally, physically, and financially.

1Corinthians 13:8 *Love never fails.*

Love, live, laugh, give and forgive, learn, create & play, savor the wonder's of God's music, art and beauty. As a nutritionist, I must admit that what you are eating is not nearly important as what is eating you. While some cancer patients recover without getting optimal nutrition, no cancer patient recovers unless their spiritual needs are met. This section is the most important in this book, or any other book.

Love. There is no greater power on earth. There are 737 references to "love" in the Bible. Jesus came to earth when the Pharisees had a long checklist of requirements for getting into heaven. Jesus saved us from that nonsense. He spoke of salvation through "grace".

John1:17 *For the law was given through Moses; grace and truth came through Jesus Christ.*

Jesus took the Pharisees lengthy rule book and reduced it to 2 simple commandments.

Matthew 22:37-9 *"'Love the Lord your God with all your heart and with all your soul and with all your mind.' This is the first and greatest commandment. And the second is like it: 'Love your neighbor as yourself.'*

Notice that we begin by loving God. We then must love others and ourselves, not instead of ourselves. You cannot give away something that you don't have. If you don't love yourself, then you can't love anyone else. Dr. Carl Jung was a celebrated Swiss psychiatrist who concluded his long and brilliant career around 1960 saying that 95% of mental illness is induced by low self-esteem—not loving yourself.

Children enthusiastically live for today, they laugh and play, they frolick and forgive easily, they create a better tomorrow by using their imagination and creative skills, they do not worry about yesterday or tomorrow. Jesus told us to "be like children". The world "enthusiasm" comes from the Greek word "enthios", meaning "God within." Enthusiastic people are filled with God's spirit and become a magnet for good things to happen in their lives. Just pretend to be enthusiastic for a few days until you get the feelings. Savor each day. Be here now. Don't anguish over the past or future.

Matthew 18:3 *And he said: "I tell you the truth, unless you change and become like little children, you will never enter the kingdom of heaven.*

Give to your church and other charities with enthusiasm. Tithe (ten percent) of your time, talents, and money. Once you are convinced of the merits of tithing, you may want to crank up your prosperity another notch by "seeding"; that is planting gifts to God so that you can reap the abundant harvest. Don't just wait for the harvest to come in and then give 10% back to God.

Luke 6:38 *Give, and it will be given to you. A good measure, pressed down, shaken together and running over, will be poured into your lap. For with the measure you use, it will be measured to you."*

Many people think that they cannot afford to give ten percent to charitable causes. Actually, we cannot afford NOT to give back to the Lord. God made it all and there is an unlimited supply of whatever. By giving back, you plant seeds for a new and bountiful harvest. Think of the simple arithmetic. Plant one seed of corn and you get about 400 seeds back in the harvest. Therefore, if you give ten percent of everything you have, you will soon be reaping an increasingly bountiful harvest. You cannot outgive God. But its fun to try.

Malachi 3:10 *"Bring the whole tithe into the storehouse, that there may be food in my house. Test me in this," says the Lord Almighty, "and see if I will not throw open the floodgates of heaven and pour out so much blessing that you will not have room enough for it."*

Forgive. Let it go. When we hold grudges, even if they are well justified, we bind that person to us. Jesus taught us how to pray with the incredibly beautiful and succinct "Our Father", in which the original Aramaic translation was "untie us from our debtors". Just picture dragging people around who you are holding a grudge against.

Matthew 6:12 *Forgive us our debts, as we also have forgiven our debtors.*

Matthew 18:21-2 *Then Peter came to Jesus and asked, "Lord, how many times shall I forgive my brother when he sins against me? Up to seven times?" Jesus answered, "I tell you, not seven times, but seventy-seven times.*

Forgiving wipes the slate clean. Holding a grudge does not hurt the person who hurt you, it only hurts you. Forgiveness can be a cleansing experience like none other.

Ephesians 4:31 *Get rid of all bitterness,*
rage and anger...

Learn with a passion. One of the greatest scientists in all of history, Albert Einstein, told us that humans use less than 10% of their mental potential. Many problems have been solved by God-given human intelligence. Think of the technological wonders that make our lives easier: phone, computers, jet travel, microwave oven, TV, radio, laser surgery, satellite communications. God has given us the potential to solve all of our problems, but it will take effort on our part to do so. Learn to help yourself. Learn to help others. Learn for the sheer joy of it!

2Chronicles 1:12 *therefore wisdom and*
knowledge will be given you. And I will also give
you wealth, riches and honor, such as no king who
was before you ever had and none after you will
have.

Create and play, sing and dance, savor the many beauties that surround you.

Jeremiah 31:13 *Then maidens will dance*
and be glad, young men and old as well. I will turn
their mourning into gladness; I will give them com-
fort and joy instead of sorrow.

Express yourself. Jesus was expressive when He whipped the money changers in the temple and wept at the Garden of Gethsemane.

Mark14:34 *My soul is overwhelmed with*
sorrow to the point of death," he said to them.
"Stay here and keep watch."

Our emotions are given to us by God as "balancing sticks to help us walk the tightrope of life". When you feel emotions, express them in a productive way: write in a journal, laugh, talk to a friend or counselor, cry, sing, dance, go into a room by yourself and pound a mattress with a pillow; but get the emotions out or they will produce some physical illness. People who hurt others, fight, and slam doors are expressing their emotions, but in a hurtful way. Americans seem to have inherited some of the

British tradition of "keeping a stiff upper lip" when problems develop. While persistence and faith are noble traits that get us through tough times, expressing our emotions in some non-destructive way is crucial for our mental and physical health.

Ecclesiastes 3:4 *a time to weep and a time to laugh, a time to mourn and a time to dance.*

Be yourself. There are no two snowflakes alike. There are no two humans alike, even between identical twins. There has never been nor will there ever be someone just like you on God's green earth. You have a unique set of skills, physical and emotional traits that allow only you to contribute to society in some distinctive way. Don't try to imitate someone else. You won't do well at being them, and you certainly will deprive the world of your unique set of skills. The robin does not envy the beaver for his ability to make dams. The robin contributes with his song and controlling the insect population. God wants you to be yourself, no one else can perform that role better than you.

Matthew 5:16 *In the same way, let your light shine before men, that they may see your good deeds and praise your Father in heaven.*

Focus on what you have and what parts of your body are working well and give thanks. Always see the glass as half full. This is not Pollyanna escapism, it is the word of God.

Philipians 4:8 *Finally, brothers, whatever is true, whatever is noble, whatever is right, whatever is pure, whatever is lovely, whatever is admirable—if anything is excellent or praiseworthy—think about such things.*

WHAT TO DO: Make sure that each day is a celebration of love and laughter. Make your life a masterpiece of God's joy. There will be plenty of times to mourn, but do not pass up the opportunities to laugh and play.

Maintain healthy blood sugar. By reducing your intake of sweet foods, you can virtually eliminate dental cavities. And by controlling rises in blood sugar, you can dramatically improve overall health through prostaglandin regulation. The amount of sugar in your blood is totally dependent on what you eat. The sugar in your blood affects insulin and glucagon, which then affect prostaglandins, which are extremely important:

† dilate blood vessels for better circulation
† improve immune readiness
† decrease the stickiness of cells to prevent strokes or spreading cancer
† help the body to make estrogen receptors to further cut cancer risk
† improve the burning of fat stores in the body.

Control your blood sugar levels through diet and supplements, and you can have a huge impact on your health. Cancer and Candida yeast cells feed on sugar. It is virtually impossible to have good health unless you can control blood sugar.

WHAT TO DO: Reduce your intake of sweet things. Try to avoid white sugar altogether, because it is more of a drug than a food. Use sweeteners as a condiment, not as a staple. Instead of white sugar, substitute honey, concentrated apple juice, barley malt, fructose, molasses, sucanat, maltose, date sugar, rice syrup, and dried fruit. Avoid artificial sweeteners, including saccharin (Equal) and aspartame (Nutrasweet). These synthetic chemicals have done nothing to reduce the incidence of obesity in America, but are likely suspects in ruining health.

If you have hypoglycemia (low blood sugar) or the opposite side of the coin (hyperglycemia), then take supplements of chromium, B-6, and zinc along with these other recommendations. These nutrients will assist insulin action. Eat nothing sweet by itself, including fruit, but rather eat sweet foods (like honey and fruit) with a mixed meal, thus moderating rises in blood glucose. The average American consumes about 132 pounds per year of sugar. Cut this down to 30-40 pounds and watch your health improve.

Nutrient density allows us to make better food choices. In the real world, food choices are limited, whether at a restaurant, on an airplane, or at your boss's house for dinner. Try to select the most nourishing foods based upon the choices available. Nutrient density is based on the amount of vitamins, minerals, protein, and fiber per hundred calories. Add in the important concept of risk versus benefit from the food; and you can choose the best of the options available.

WHAT TO DO: Study the following chart and become familiar with this concept of nutrient density, which will allow you to eat just about anywhere and make the best possible selections.

RATING YOUR FOODS

Based on "risk versus benefit" and "nutrient density" (i.e. vitamins, minerals, fiber, & protein per 100 calories) the following foods have been judged from "best" to "worst" for the average healthy adult. Eat foods high on the chart.

BEST

oranges	beet greens	brussel sprouts	parsley	garlic	barley	bass
limes	cauliflower	dandelion	greens	cabbage	green peppers	wheat
halibut	tangerine	tomato	chard	endive	carrots	oats
sole	banana	asparagus	pumpkin	sprouts	black eyed	whole grain
cod	strawberries	low fat yogurt	winter squash	kale	peas	bread
haddock	cantaloupe	nonfat milk	sweet potatoes	pinto beans	wheat germ	millet
octopus	guava	buttermilk	turnip greens	soybeans	brewer's yeast	amaranth
apricot	spinach	garbanzo	brown rice	spirulina	papaya	onions
beans	rye	navy beans				

GOOD

cherries	low fat milk	lettuce	low fat beef,	trout	ginger	blueberries
low fat	peas	tuna	pork, veal,	chicory	grapes	parmesan
cheese	lima beans	swordfish	lamb	cinnamon	honeydew	potatoes
corn	clams	turkey	melon	radishes	popcorn	oysters
chicken	watermelon	zucchini	grits	abalone	kidney	pineapple
celery	tortilla	lobster	heart	apple	beets	green tea
shrimp	eggs	pear	hot peppers	salmon	liver	vinegar

FAIR

prunes	walnuts	homemade pizza &	raisins	vegetable juice
whole milk	peanuts	whole wheat crust	dates	sesame seeds
high fat beef,	homemade low	most cheeses	duck	almonds
pork, veal	fat granola	plums	rhubarb	
whole wheat &	pumpkin seeds	sunflower seeds	fruit juice	
fresh fruit pie	peanut butter	dried fruit		

POOR

molasses	ice cream	white rice	honey	soy, corn, olive,
commercial pizza	sweetened	commercial granola	crackers	safflower, sunflower,
canned fruit	condensed milk	pancakes	avocado	cottonseed oils
waffles	white flour	creamed vegetables	white noodles	

BAD

sausage	sugar	commercial pies	cake	sugared breakfast
hotdog	wine	corn chips	syrup	cereals
bacon	beer	gelatin desserts	butter	salami
tea	mayonnaise	coconut	coffee	ketchup
vinegar &	diet soft	spices	bologna	
oil salad	drinks			
dressings				

WORST

pastries	distilled spirits	lard	doughnuts	soft drinks
mayonnaise &	salt	olives	pretzels	monosodium
blue cheese	potato chips	hydrogenated fat	pickles	glutamate
salad dressings	stick margarine	soup mixes		

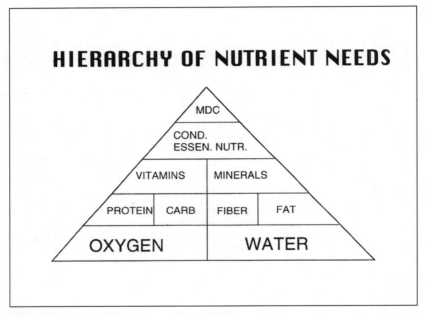

HIERARCHY OF NUTRIENT NEEDS

Oxygen is the most essential nutrient in the human body. We can live weeks or even months without food, a few days without water, but only a few minutes without oxygen. While the letter "A" spoke of anti-oxidants, or nutrients that protect us from oxidative stress, we are also aerobic creatures who must have optimal amounts of oxygen in order for all bodily systems to work properly. Poorly oxygenated tissue will slowly starve and shut down organ efficiency, increase the buildup of yeast and cancer (since these two life forms do not need much oxygen) and change the pH (acid/base) balance in the body.

WHAT TO DO: Breathing techniques are critical. Deep belly breathing, often called diaphragm breathing, allows us to draw oxygen into the deep recesses of the lungs to fully oxygenate the body. Lie on the floor with a book on your stomach. Begin your breathing rhythm by pushing the book toward the ceiling using stomach muscles to push out, next continue inhaling by filling up the rib cage. Exhale in the opposite order.

To fully oxygenate the body, exercise at least 30 minutes each day. While one out of three Americans will develop cancer, only one out of seven active Americans will get cancer. One of the best exercises is vigorous walking, because you need no partner, no special equipment beyond decent shoes, nearly any weather will do, and nearly anyone can do it for the rest of their lives.

Also, complex carbohydrate foods, such as grains, beans, vegetables, and fruit provide a better oxygen quotient in the tissue than fats. Take a B-complex supplement, chromium, and Coenzyme Q to further enrich the body with oxygen. Obviously, avoid air polluted areas and smoking.

> Genesis 2:7 *the LORD God formed the man from the dust of the ground and breathed into his nostrils the breath of life, and the man became a living being.*

Purify your body, mind, and spirit. There are spiritual poisons of doubt, hate, vengeance, hopelessness, depression, pessimism, and low self esteem. There are physical poisons, both involuntary (such as air, water, and food pollution) and voluntary (like tobacco, alcohol, and drugs). All of these toxins will poison the body and sap us of life. Americans dumps 90 billion pounds of toxic waste into our 55,000 toxic waste sites, we add another 1.2 billion pounds of pesticides to our food supply, and then expose ourselves to frightening levels of toxic metals and chemicals from industry and agriculture.

WHAT TO DO: Stop the ingestion of all kinds of poisons. Drink filtered water. Help clean up God's planet that we steward. Help the body to eliminate the accumulated waste products via feces, urine, and sweat.

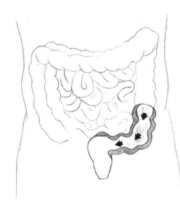

Increase your intake of water and fiber to purge the colon. Hyssop is a purgative herb mentioned often in the Bible. Use it for cleansing. Increase intake of water, vitamin C, selenium, and the amino acids methionine and cysteine to improve excretion of waste products through the urine. Take hot tubs, hot showers, saunas, and exercise to cleanse the skin pores. You may need to exchange your mercury fillings for non-metallic composites. Depending on the dust and pollen level in your area, you may find great relief in using the

"nasal purge", which mixes 1/2 teaspoon of sea salt into 1 cup of lukewarm water, then slowly draw the salt water solution up into the sinuses, hold it, then expel it. This technique helps to cleanse a major area of irritation.

Psalms 51:7 *Cleanse me with hyssop, and I will be clean; wash me, and I will be whiter than snow.*

Quiet time. Prayer and relaxation are absolutely essential for spiritual, mental, financial, and physical health. Psychologists tell us that much stress and premature aging are induced by people whose minds are always cluttered. We have a biological need to still the mind and dwell on God.

Psalms 46:10 *Be still, and know that I am God*

WHAT TO DO: Take some time each day to get in a dark room, get comfortable, relax all of your muscles through some slow deep breathing, then focus on God and only God. If a thought keeps disturbing your focus, then write it down and continue. Daily, take mini-vacations in which you get still and picture a very relaxing scene for 5 to 10 minutes. The more vivid you can imagine this relaxing scene, the more beneficial the results.

Psalm 23 *He makes me lie down in green pastures,*
he leads me beside still waters, he restores my soul.

Real world eating includes tolerance and forgiveness, which allows healthy people to eat 90% nourishing food and 10% other food. Consider the 10% "other" food to be sacrificial and even "medicinal". If you are celebrating your grandmother's 80th birthday and she baked a cake for everyone, then eat it. Don't tell her you are off sweets. When 90% of your food intake is nourishing, then you can tolerate, and perhaps even need, the

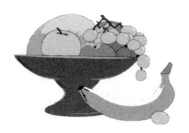

other 10% "junk food" that won't matter to your healthy body. Eat to live, do not live to eat.

WHAT TO DO: Make every effort to buy, prepare, and select nourishing foods. The sacrificial 10% will come your way without having to look for it.

Small frequent meals. God designed us as "grazers", not the "gorgers" that we have become. We can better avoid heart disease, diabetes, obesity, and gastro-intestinal problems when we "snack" our way through the day.

WHAT TO DO: Eat a small but nourishing breakfast. I usually have a mixed drink of pureed fruits and vegetables along with powdered protein and vitamins, plus whole grain bread, and fresh fruit. Eat a small snack at mid-morning. You can bring whole grain ready-to-eat cereals with you to the office, like Shredded Wheat, Cheerios, and Wheaties. Eat a modest lunch. Take half of your lunch and eat it at mid-afternoon. This program will help to eliminate binge eating.

Thyroid monitoring. According to Dr. Broda Barnes, a noted physician and researcher, 40% of Americans are suffering from low thyroid function. One of the more important yet least known aspects of good health is an active thyroid gland. Located in the neck region, the thyroid gland is often called the "master gland" because it regulates the rate at which we burn food for energy. Since all cells need energy all of the time, this becomes a pretty important index. Though laboratory tests check the levels of Thyroid Stimulating Hormone (TSH) in the blood, a much more accurate means of assessing thyroid function is to check your body temperature first thing in the morning. If your temperature and thyroid function are low, then the symptoms include: inability to lose weight, poor mental and physical energy levels, being cold often, frequent constipation, and sexual problems (painful or excessive menstruation, infertility, impotency, low libido). Over the long run, these annoying symptoms deteriorate into heart disease, increased infections, hypoglycemia, mental disturbances, cancer, poor digestion, and more. Do not procrastinate and let this problem continue.

WHAT TO DO: Using a digital thermometer, take your temperature first thing in the morning before moving or getting anything to drink. If you average less than 97.8 F over the course of several days, then you may be suffering from low thyroid. If so, first try natural methods to "jump start" the thyroid gland with one or all of the following:

    † take 6 tablets of sea kelp daily

    † twice daily on an empty stomach take 2 grams of tyrosine plus 4 drops (about 300 mcg) of liquid kelp (rich in iodine)

    † 15 drops twice daily of bladderwrack (an herb that helps thyroid function).

If 3 months of trying these methods fails to get your morning temperature up to at least 97.8 F, then see your family physician for a prescription of dessicated natural thyroid.

Understand the importance of 7 F's. In order of importance: faith, family, fun, feelings, food, fitness, and finances. Keep your attention focused on these important factors in your life and all else will take care of itself. Turn your life into an enviable masterpiece. If Christians live the life that God wants us to have, then other people will ask you "what is your secret to happiness?", at which time you can readily share the Gospel of Jesus Christ. However, if your life is not working, then do not export it to others.

WHAT TO DO: Dwell on the important 7 F's in life, and keep them in the proper priority.

Vitamin supplements can be valuable when used in addition to, rather than instead of, good eating. Before the dawn of stress and pollutants and eating on the run, vitamin and mineral supplements were probably not important. But in America, nutritional supplements can make a major difference

between "surviving" and "thriving". For as little as $20 per month per person, one can have a high quality, broad spectrum, bioavailable vitamin and mineral supplement that will cut the risk for diseases while slowing the aging process.

Reasons Why Nutritional Supplementation May be Beneficial

1. We do not eat well. Extensive food surveys show that 92% of Americans do not receive the Recommended Dietary Allowance (RDA) for all nutrients.

2. Difference between "surviving" and "thriving". The RDA does not provide for optimal health. While the RDA for vitamin E is 10 mg/day, which most people get, 200 mg/day will cut heart disease risks by 40%, while 800 mg/day (80 times the RDA) will improve immune functions.

3. Mineral-depleted soil. Since commercial farming does not add trace minerals (like selenium and chromium) back to the soil, and since humans have more complex mineral requirements than plants, our fresh produce has less minerals.

4. Stress depletes nutrient reserves. Both physical and psychological stress increase the need for various nutrients.

5. Exposure to toxins. Agricultural and industrial pollutants in the air, food, and water supply increase the need for various nutrients.

6. Help reverse diseases. Coupled with other therapies, vitamins, minerals, herbs, amino acids, and other food extracts can improve the body's ability to recover from diseases.

WHAT TO DO: Go to your local health food store, or call one of the vitamin companies listed in the appendix of this book. Buy a good broad spectrum vitamin and mineral supplement. Chelated (say "key-lated") minerals are better absorbed than mineral salts. While natural vitamins may be more effective than synthetic vitamins, natural vitamins are less dense and more costly which makes them impractical for concentrating into pill form. You may want to use other nutrients for other purposes. For instance, herbs, like ginseng, are adaptogens, which improve overall functions in the body. Though these herbs are not essential, they do bring health up a notch. Other valuable supplements include:

† Lactobacillus, especially for people who do not eat yogurt regularly

† herbs that stimulate immune function, like echinacea, goldenseal, licorice, etc.

† herbs that improve circulation, like ginkgo biloba

† amino acids to improve mental functions, like tyrosine

† lecithin to help clear out the arteries and feed the brain

† others, as directed by your health care professional

Remember, nutritional supplements are far safer and cheaper than drugs, but if used carelessly, even God's gentle healers in nature can create toxicity or imbalances.

Water. Both the earth's surface and the human body are two thirds water. Up to 90% of the fruits and vegetables we eat are water. Water is an amazing substance:

† essential for digestion

† the prime solvent in the body and is the medium of the blood

† bathes our eyes and mouth to wipe away bacteria from the environment

† provides both lubrication and traction

† flushes impurities out of the
   system
† helps to maintain proper acid/base
balance.

Yet most Americans walk around in a constant state of dehy-
dration. If you have dry or wrinkled skin, frequent constipation,
clouded mind, and frequent infections, then your problem may
be as simple as drinking more clean water. Though we can sur-
vive when we are a couple of pints low in body water, we can
only thrive when these pints are replenished.

WHAT TO DO: Consume lots of clean water daily.
Depending on your size, activity, climate, and food intake of
water—8 to 16 glasses of water should quench the long standing thirst that keeps many people continuously ill. Though fruit
juice and tea count as fluid intake, it is also critical to get a certain percentage of your fluid intake as pure water; from uncont-
aminated springs, or filtered through reverse osmosis, carbon
block, or distillation.

Exercise. God designed humans to be active
creatures. With regular exercise, we:
   † keep our appetite under control
   † improve both mental alertness and
      tranquility; no drug can do both at
      the same time
   † massage the food through the
      intestines for regularity
   † clear fats out of the bloodstream
   † stabilize blood glucose levels

† improve toxin excretion

† and generally improve circulation to feed all of the distant tissue.

There is no cheaper or more effective prescription for every man, woman, and child, than 30 minutes of vigorous movement each day. Kids become calmer and are better students. Adults work better, play better, and sleep better.

WHAT TO DO: Start each day with at least 10 minutes of prayer, followed by at least 20 minutes of exercise. This simple half hour expenditure of time will improve your life a thousand fold. Brisk walking is the easiest thing to do for a lifetime. Don't forget about chores that actually accomplish something; including mowing the lawn, working in the garden, kneading bread, etc. Actually, the single most calorie-intensive exercise of all is woodchopping. Work toward flexibility, strength, and aerobic condition (endurance). If your resting morning pulse is at or below 60 beats per minute, then you are getting enough exercise and sparing the heart of the 50% more wear and tear which happens in someone who is less fit.

Y

Yes to superfoods. See chapter 2 for these Bible foods that bring extra nourishment and should be included in your diet often. Simple changes in the diet can bring huge rewards in health. For instance, carrots are so rich in beta-carotene, which stimulates immune function and protects against free radicals, that if Americans did nothing different except eat 2 extra carrots each day, then we could cut cancer incidence by 300,000 peo-

ple each year. Each of these superfoods has the potential of making a huge beneficial impact on your health.

WHAT TO DO: Eat these foods often: carrots, yogurt, cabbage family (broccoli, cauliflower, brussel sprouts), garlic & onion, ocean fish (i.e., halibut, salmon, tuna), dark green leafy vegetables (i.e., collards, spinach, beet greens), green and orange fruits and vegetables (i.e., yams, apricots, peas), foods high in soluble fiber (i.e., bananas, apples, carrots, seaweed). Get creative in the kitchen. Try some new recipes and cookbooks. See the appendix for recommendations. See chapter 6 for some recipe suggestions and a one week menu plan which emphasizes these super foods.

Zoo animals eat their God-given diet—shouldn't we? Walk through a big city zoo and feast your eyes on the incredible diversity that God has created on earth. Each of these creatures has a God-given diet that is crucial to its health. Ask any veterinarian about the importance of diet for an animal's health. If zoo keepers deviate even slightly from the indigenous diet that an animal is supposed to get, then the animal will get sick. Humans, too, have a God-given diet, which we have deviated from substantially and have paid the price for our disobedience to God's laws.

WHAT TO DO: Eat what God has outlined for you in Holy Scripture, and what is meant to keep you in good health for the better part of a century. Eat God's life-giving food, not mankind's dead and adulterated food. Know that God wants you to be healthy, but you have to do your part to earn that health.

Personal Profile

PN was a successful business man who took good care of himself. He dedicated time each day to exercise, prayer, and eating properly. He did not smoke and rarely drank any alcohol. But he was having a terrible time with asthma. A few physicians had recommended that he get a good air filtration system and hide in his house, office, and car for the bulk of the year. PN was not willing to make such a sacrifice, since he enjoyed outdoor activities, including biking, tennis, boating, and golf. Medication did not help relieve the shortness of breath.

I recommended that PN take supplements of extra magnesium, vitamin C, rutin, and the herbs ginseng, diascorea, licorice (glycyrrhiza glabra), rhodiola, and schizandra. This program helped tremendously, but when we later added lobelia (liquid tincture allowed to run down the esophagus), PN felt better than he had in years. He can now enjoy his favorite outdoor sports while breathing fully.

CHAPTER 4

◆

COMPACT GUIDE TO NUTRITIONAL & HERBAL MEDICINE

USING GOD'S GENTLE HEALERS

IMPORTANT NOTE: These supplements are to be monitored by your trained health care professional!! Unless otherwise stated, all amino acids are L form and all supplements are to be taken orally.

1Chronicles 22:13 *Then you will have success if you are careful to observe the decrees and laws that the LORD gave Moses for Israel.*

Personal Profile

BF was a single mother of 3 children, all of whom were having major health problems. She also was suffering financially from the 20% co-payment on her health insurance policy, thus stretching BF's marginal paycheck beyond its capacity to support her family. She needed health help and she hoped that it would be cheaper than what she was paying for drugs and doctor bills.

BF suffered from chronic yeast infections and fatigue. The oldest child, TF, was grappling with teenage acne and the many side effects from Accutane medication. LF was the athlete in the family who was having trouble keeping her weight up with all the running she was doing. JF was the youngest in the family and she suffered from chronic ear infections.

BF was put on a diet similar to the one listed in the menu plan chapter of this book. She found it tolerable in the begin-

ning and liked it within a month. I asked her to add one full bulb of garlic to each dinner meal, prepared according to the directions in the menu plan chapter. We also added 1 cup of lowfat active cultured yogurt to her daily diet. In addition to her multiple vitamin and mineral supplement, she also took extra vitamin C, E, beta-carotene, B-6, and zinc. In my discussions with her, it was clear that her recent ugly divorce had left many emotional scars. I asked her to see a counselor who could help her to express her anger, grief, and loss and then begin the forgiveness and healing process. Dealing with emotional pain is not easy, but she did it and looked like a completely different person within 6 months. She also began dating a wonderful man who treated her well, unlike her former husband's abuse.

As for the children, TF was put on a low fat diet that excluded all dairy products, including his favorite pizza. I asked him to take a multiple vitamin and mineral supplement, plus extra vitamin A from fish oil, zinc, chromium polynicotinate, and fish oil capsules. He also began cleansing his face daily, getting 20 minutes of sun exposure daily, and keeping his hands away from his face, which had become a nervous habit. He elected to stop his medication and follow this program. Within 2 months his acne was gone.

LF was a growing 14 year old woman who loved to run cross country. Because she ran so much and did not eat right, her body fat was so low that she had not begun her menstruation like most of her friends. I explained to her that God has a plan; if you don't have enough body fat to carry through a pregnancy, then the body will not release eggs for a woman's normal monthly menstruation cycle. She understood the need to allow God's plan to unfold in her life and body. She began a program of morning "shakes" containing home made yogurt and powdered protein. She also agreed to start eating meals regularly. She began taking a multiple vitamin and mineral supplement plus extra zinc, and found that her appetite picked up considerably. Within 6 months, she was at a good weight, had become the top freshman cross-country runner at her school, and also began her healthy menstrual periods.

JF was struggling with depression from her parent's divorce. I asked the mother, BF, to bring the family to counselling to begin the healing process of a splintered family. I also recom-

mended that JF start taking chewable vitamins, since she was only 5 years old. We were also able to get some powdered vitamin C in her breakfast orange juice. She took a homeopathic preparation for chronic ear infections. All of which helped to cut the incidence and severity of her ear infections within the next 2 months. But when her 2 baby teeth with mercury fillings fell out, her ear aches completely ceased. Mercury is a known poison which may affect many people who have mercury dental fillings causing allergies, depression, increased infections, and more.

You may recall that BF came to me initially with both health and finance problems. When I made recommendations regarding food choices and supplements, she responded with "we can't afford that stuff." I mentioned that if she invested a little today, she would reap a major savings in doctor's bills later. She now reports that fresh and nourishing food has cut their grocery bills by 20%, while their several thousand dollars spent annually on doctor bills is now down to about $500 each year spent on vitamin and herbal supplements for the whole family.

There are thousands of good scientific studies showing that vitamins, minerals, amino acids, herbs, and other nutrition compounds can be very therapeutic in healing health problems. See the appendix for mail order companies who sell these products. The following directory has been condensed from many studies and some excellent reference books, including:

Anderson, WELLNESS MEDICINE, Keats, 1987
Balch & Balch, PRESCRIPTION FOR NUTRITIONAL HEALING, Avery, 1993
Grabowski, RJ, CURRENT NUTRITIONAL THERAPY, Image Press, 1993
Hausman, THE RIGHT DOSE, Rodale, 1987
Hendler, DOCTOR'S VITAMIN AND MINERAL ENCYCLOPEDIA, Simon & Schuster,1990
Lieberman, S. et al., REAL VITAMIN & MINERAL BOOK, Avery, 1990
Murray, M, et al., ENCYCLOPEDIA OF NATURAL MEDICINE, Prima, 1990
Quillin, P., HEALING NUTRIENTS, Random House, 1987
Werbach, M, NUTRITIONAL INFLUENCES ON ILLNESS, Third Line, 1993

FOR THIS DISORDER	USE THESE NUTRITIONAL & HERBAL HEALERS
acne	*no iodine or kelp, use chromium, brewer's yeast, lecithin, zinc, selenium, A, E, B-6, folacin, low fat & sugar diet, fish or flax oil, chaste berry, gugulipid, topical tea tree oil, alfalfa, burdock, cayenne, dandelion root, echinacea, red clover*
AIDS	*garlic, Lactobacillus, C, E, B-complex, B-12, B-6, A, CoQ, zinc, thymus, selenium, chromium, calcium, magnesium, potassium, arginine, glutathione, cysteine, enzymes, fish or flax oil, aloe vera, bloodroot, celandine, garlic, licorice, St. John's Wort, trichosanthin, silymarin, cayenne, echinacea, ginseng, goldenseal, Pau d'arco, ginkgo, maitake, quercetin*
alcoholism	*no extra A; use B-complex, B-1, B-2, B-3, B-6, B-12, C & bioflavonoids (catechin), E, D, folacin, pantothenate, borage or primrose oil, glutamine, taurine, carnitine, tryptophan, calcium, potassium, magnesium, selenium, free form amino acids, choline, lecithin, kudzu, gotu kola, berberine, valerian, kava, silymarin*
allergies	*allergy detection (find & eliminate the offending foods), B-3, B-12 sublingual, C, E, selenium, zinc, calcium, magnesium, enzymes, pantothenate, quercetin, bee pollen, Lactobacillus, feverfew, garlic, ginkgo, stinging nettles, burdock, dandelion, goldenseal, centaury, ginseng, astragalus, phytolacca*

FOR THIS DISORDER	USE THESE NUTRITIONAL & HERBAL HEALERS
Alzheimer's	*(including dementia & senility): C, E, beta-carotene, niacin, selenium, zinc, potassium, CoQ, lecithin, kelp, DNA/RNA, ginkgo, butcher's broom*
anemia	*liver extract, chelated iron, folate, A, C, E, B-1, B-2, B-6, B-12, pan-thothenate, zinc, copper, alfalfa, dandelion, mullen, nettle, red raspberry*
anorexia	*high dose multiple vitamin & mineral formula, zinc, potassium, magnesium, kava, valerian, St. John's wort*
anxiety	*(see also hypoglycemia), no alcohol or caffeine, use chromium, B-3, B-6, GABA, glutamine, melatonin, Ashwagandha, valerian, kava, hops, catnip, chamomile, passion flower, melissa, Panax ginseng, ginkgo, skullcap, Suanzaorentang (Chinese herbal mix), deep breathing, lots of purified water*
arthritis	*(including rheumatoid, osteo, rheumatism): vegetarian diet; fish, primrose, flax, & borage oils; enzymes (bromelain & Wobenzyme), glucosamine sulfate, cartilage extract, sulfur, calcium, magnesium, boron, copper, zinc, selenium, iron, gold, C & bioflavonoids (quercetin, catechin), E, K, pantothenate, B-3, B-6, folacin, CoQ, DL-phenylalanine, tryptophan, histidine, garlic, allergy detection, sea cucumber (Beche-de-Mer),*

FOR THIS DISORDER	USE THESE NUTRITIONAL & HERBAL HEALERS
	Boswellia serrata, green-lipped mussel (perna canaliculus), alfalfa, black cohosh, ginger, curcumin, topical cayenne (capsaicin), DMSO, celery seed, devil's claw, feverfew, parsley, valerian, yucca (saponin extract), Phytodolor N (Germany herb mix)
asthma	*selenium, calcium, magnesium, D, C, A, B-3, B-6, quercetin, pantothenate, allergy detection, low sodium diet, cysteine; fish or flax oils; bee pollen, aloe vera, Coleus (Ayurvedic mix), Galphimia glauca, ginkgo, Khella, lobelia, onion, Picrorrhiza kurroa, Tylophora asthmatica, echinacea, horsetail, juniper berries, licorice, gotu kola, caffeine, MaHuang, Pau D'arco, propolis, slippery elm*
auto-immune disorders	*(including lupus, multiple sclerosis, rheumatoid arthritis, scleroderma, myopathy, vitiligo, etc): allergy detection, detoxification, calcium, magnesium, selenium, zinc, enzymes, garlic, C, A, beta-carotene, E, B-3, B-6, B-12, pantothenate, selenium, sulfur; fish, borage, primrose & flax oils; ginseng, astragalus, silymarin, alfalfa, Tripterygium wilfordi, ginkgo, Khella, Psoralea coryliforia (India herb mix), Padma (Tibet herb mix), echinacea, licorice, goldenseal, pau d'arco, yucca*

FOR THIS DISORDER	USE THESE NUTRITIONAL & HERBAL HEALERS
backache	calcium, magnesium, DL-phenylalanine, enzymes, burdock, horsetail, white willow, topical DMSO
bedsores	E, A, beta-carotene, protein, zinc, copper, garlic, kelp, goldenseal, myrrh, topical aloe
bed-wetting	vegetable protein, calcium, magnesium, potassium, flax or fish oil, buchu, corn silk, oat straw, parsley, plantain, allergy detection, less liquids at bedtime
benign breast disease:	avoid coffee, tea, cola, & chocolate; use low fat diet, A, E, iodine, primrose oil
bladder infection	Lactobacillus, C, E, beta-carotene, zinc, selenium, thymus, garlic, cranberry, burdock, juniper, marshmellow root, rose hips, goldenseal, lots of water
bronchitis	C, bioflavonoids (rutin, quercetin, proanthocyanidins), beta-carotene, vitamin A from fish oil, E, garlic, zinc, CoQ, arginine, black radish, chickweed, coltsfoot, echinacea, eucalyptus, fenugreek, ginger, myrrh, slippery elm bark
bruising	C, E, bioflavonoids (rutin), alfalfa, protein, zinc, enzymes, alfalfa, garlic, rose hips
burns	protein, C, E, A, D, potassium, magnesium, fish or flax oil; poultice of

FOR THIS DISORDER	USE THESE NUTRITIONAL & HERBAL HEALERS
	aloe, sumac, sweet gum, white oak bark, blackberry leaves
cancer	multi-vitamin & mineral, diet low in fat & sugar & rich in plant food, soy, C & bioflavonoids (quercetin, catechin, pycnogenol), D, K, E succinate, B-1, B-2, B-3, B-6, B-12, folacin, A, beta-carotene, zinc, selenium, chromium, potassium, iodine, flax & fish oil, enzymes & bromelain, garlic, maitake & Shitake, PSK (cloud fungus mushroom), seaweed, aloe vera, thymus, enzymes, CoQ, shark oil, cartilage extract, arginine, cysteine, glutamine, Lactobacillus, tumeric, Ukrain (Chelidonium Majus L.), aloe, benzaldehyde (in almond oil), berberine, Carnivora (Venus fly trap), Chaparral, Chlorella, Coumarin (herbal mix), echinacea, pau d'arco, astragalus, goldenseal, licorice, Mistletoe, Panax ginseng, Essiac, Hoxsey
candidiasis	low sugar diet, caprylic acid, Lugol's iodine, garlic, B-2, B-6, C, E, A, beta-carotene, copper, iron, magnesium, selenium, fish & flax oil, Lactobacillus, garlic, yogurt, yogurt douche, undecylenic acid, berberine, cassia alata (ringworm senna), tea tree oil vaginal suppository, echinacea, pau d'arco, clove, black walnut, wormwood, detoxification
canker sores	Lactobacillus, lysine, garlic, A, E, folacin, B-12, beta-carotene, iron,

FOR THIS DISORDER	USE THESE NUTRITIONAL & HERBAL HEALERS
	zinc lozenge, Longo Vital (herbal mix), topical Melissa (lemon balm) or licorice
carpal tunnel syndrome	*B-2, B-6*
cataracts	*multi-vitamin & mineral, C & bioflavonoids, E, B-2, B-3, folacin, beta-carotene, D, E, A & eye drops of A, calcium, magnesium, copper, zinc, selenium, cysteine, methionine, taurine, DMG, low sugar & dairy diet, ginkgo, bilberry, Hachimijiogan (Chinese herbal mix), eye bright herb*
cervical dysplasia	*folacin, A, beta-carotene, C, E, sele-nium*
chronic fatigue syndrome	*B-12 sub-lingual, C, E, A, beta-carotene, CoQ, selenium, zinc, magnesium, potassium, bioflavonoids, Lactobacillus, fish & flax oil, germanium, enzymes, garlic, barley green, thymus, echinacea, goldenseal*
cold sores	*(herpes simplex I): topical use of: lysine, lemon balm, E, zinc sulfate; oral use of zinc lozenge, aci-dophilus, garlic, A, C & bioflavonoids, magnesium, iron, goldenseal, licorice, echinacea, no arginine (from nuts)*
colitis	*Lactobacillus, enzymes, psyllium, A, E, alfalfa, chamomile, dandelion, garlic, papaya, red clover, yarrow extract*

FOR THIS DISORDER	USE THESE NUTRITIONAL & HERBAL HEALERS
common cold	*A, beta-carotene, C, E, garlic, zinc lozenge, arginine, thymus, echinacea, goldenseal, licorice, ginger, pau d'arco, slippery elm, while willow bark, yarrow*
constipation	*fiber, psyllium, pectin, wheat bran, oat bran, folacin, pantothenate, magnesium, Lactobacillus, senna, angelica, citrus seed extract, pau d'arco*
Crohn's	*high fiber & low sugar diet, folacin, pantothenate, B-1, B-2, B-6, B-12, A, C, D, E, K, calcium, iron, magnesium, selenium, zinc, butyric acid, glycosaminoglycans, Lactobacillus, allergy detection*
dandruff	*primrose, borage, fish & flax oils; kelp, B-6, E, zinc, dandelion, goldenseal*
depression	*C plus rutin; B complex plus extra B-3, B-12 & B-6; choline or lecithin, tyrosine, magnesium, chromium, zinc, RNA, GABA; fish, borage, primrose or flax oil; ginseng, ginkgo, St. John's wort*
dermatitis	*B complex plus extra B-6, kelp, zinc, protein; fish, borage, & flax oils; A, D, E, aloe vera, allergy detection, dandelion, myrrh gum, pau d'arco*
diabetes	*lower body fat, diet low in fat & sugar & rich in fiber & complex carbohydrates, glucomannan, guar*

FOR THIS DISORDER	USE THESE NUTRITIONAL & HERBAL HEALERS
	gum, oat gum, pea fiber, pectin, psyllium, carnitine, glutathione, calcium, chromium, magnesium, copper, manganese, phosphorus, potassium, A, E, C & bioflavonoids (proanthocyanidins), B-1, B-3, B-6, biotin, CoQ, inositol; fish, borage & flax oils; brewer's yeast, enzymes with meals, ginseng, aloe, bilberry, bitter melon, cayenne (capsaicin), fenugreek, garlic, ginkgo, Gymnema sylvestre, inulin (burdock & dandelion), prickle-pear cactus, huckleberry, buchu leaves, dandelion root, goldenseal, uva ursi, chicory
diarrhea	*B-3, B-12, folacin, C, K, potassium, sodium, zinc, high protein diet, charcoal tablets, honey, Lactobacillus, glutamine, yogurt, psyllium, milk enema, kelp, potassium, fish or flax oil, multi-vitamin mineral, berberine, roasted carob powder, citrus seed extract, blackberry root, chamomile*
diverticulitis	*oat bran, psyllium, enzymes, calcium, Lactobacillus, K, E, A, alfalfa, aloe; flax, borage, or fish oil; cayenne, chamomile, garlic, papaya, yarrow*
dysmenorrhea	*(painful menstruation): A, B-3, B-6, E, iron, magnesium; fish, flax, borage or primrose oils; thyroid check, bilberry, bromelain & papain (enzymes), dong quai, feverfew,*
eczema	*A, C, D, iron, selenium, zinc; fish, flax, borage or primrose oils; allergy*

FOR THIS DISORDER	USE THESE NUTRITIONAL & HERBAL HEALERS
	detection, Euphorbia acaulis (Ayurvedic mix), ginkgo; topical use of aloe, chamomile, licorice, lupine seed extract or witch hazel
edema	*(fluid retention): protein, magnesium, low salt diet, potassium, calcium, cornsilk, B-6, C & bioflavonoids, E, alfalfa, enzymes, butcher leaves, dandelion root, garlic, horsetail, juniper berries, kelp*
emphysema	*CoQ, chlorophyll, barley green, garlic, protein, A, C, E, thymus, magnesium, calcium, kelp, fenugreek, horseradish, mullein tea, rosemary, thyme*
endometriosis	*E, iron, folacin, B-12, B-6, C & bioflavonoids (rutin, proanthocyanidins), calcium, magnesium, kelp, dong quai, raspberry leaves, ginseng, low sugar diet, allergy detection*
epilepsy	*high fat diet, taurine, tyrosine, GABA, potassium, magnesium, calcium, selenium, zinc, copper, manganese, D, E, B-1, B-3, B-6, B-12 lozenge, folacin, biotin, choline, DMG, D, L glutamic acid, primrose oil; thyroid check, enzymes, kelp, black cohosh, hyssop, lobelia, diet low in salicylates, aspartame, & additives*
fatigue	*iron, chromium, magnesium, potassium, zinc, aspartic acid, glutamine,*

FOR THIS DISORDER	USE THESE NUTRITIONAL & HERBAL HEALERS
	inosine, allergy detection, brewer's yeast, C, B complex, B-12 sub-lingual, pantothenate, folacin, chelated iron, liver extract, bee pollen, wheat germ oil, ginseng, cayenne, ginkgo, gotu kola, guarana, mahuang
gallstones	reduce body fat, diet low in fat & high in fiber, use alfalfa, lecithin, enzymes, C, E, A, choline, flax & fish oils, taurine, lemon, curcumin, silymarin, Rowachol (plant mix), peppermint oil, fennel, ginger, parsley, horsetail
glaucoma	no hydrogenated fats or caffeine; use C & rutin, chromium, zinc, topical Coleus forskohlii (Ayurvedic mix), ginkgo, Salvia militiorrhiza (Chinese herb mix)
gout	low fat vegetarian diet; no meat, gravy, beans or alcohol; use B complex, folacin, C, kelp, zinc, magnesium, birch, hyssop
hay fever	no dairy; use A, C, E, rutin, quercetin, enzymes, zinc, selenium, alfalfa, ginseng, licorice, bee pollen, detoxification
headache	(see also hypoglycemia) magnesium, calcium, potassium, ginkgo, feverfew, B-3, B-6, CoQ, choline, brigham, burdock, goldenseal, lavender, lobelia, marshmallow, mint, rosemary, cayenne ointment

FOR THIS DISORDER	USE THESE NUTRITIONAL & HERBAL HEALERS
	(capsaicin), ginger; no tyramines (from cheese & wine)
heart disease	*(including cardiac arrhythmia, atherosclerosis, thrombophlebitis, arteriosclerosis, high cholesterol): lower body fat, diet low in sugar & fat & high in fiber, vegetarian diet, garlic & onion, yogurt, lecithin, carnitine, arginine, taurine, E, C & bioflavonoids (proanthocyanidins, pycnogenol), D, beta-carotene, inositol, folacin, B-3, B-6, B-12, CoQ, calcium, magnesium, zinc, selenium, potassium, copper, fish or flax oil, rice bran (gamma oryzanol), beans or oat bran, pectin, psyllium, alfalfa, artichoke (Cynara scolymus), berberine, bilberry, bromelain & enzymes, butcher's broom, curcumin, eggplant , fenugreek, cayenne, ginger, chickweed, ginkgo, gugulipid, Khella (Ammi Visnaga), Garcinia cambogia, Centella asiatica, horsechestnut, hawthorne, silymarin, Coleus forskohlii & Abana (Ayurvedic mixes), Padma (Tibetan herb mix), activated charcoal*
heartburn	*avoid alcohol, chocolate, coffee, fatty meals, milk, orange juice, spicy foods, sugar, tea, & tomato; use aloe vera juice, licorice, A, E, enzymes, raw potato juice, water*
hemorrhoids	*psyllium, sena, magnesium, C, buckthorn, parsley, red grape vine leaves, elderberry poultice, topical E*

FOR THIS DISORDER	USE THESE NUTRITIONAL & HERBAL HEALERS
hepatitis	*thymus, silymarin, liver extract, B-12, folacin, lecithin, A, E, C & bioflavonoids (catechin), garlic, CoQ, calcium, selenium, free form amino acids, methionine, taurine, green tea, choline; borage, flax, or fish oils; licorice, Phyllanthus amarus, silymarin, Padma (Tibetan herb mix), Shosaikoto, black radish, dandelion, goldenseal*
high blood pressure	*(hypertension): vegetarian diet low in sodium, fat, sugar, alcohol, & caffeine; use potassium, calcium, magnesium, zinc, copper, taurine, tryptophan, CoQ, garlic, A, C, D, B-3, lecithin, enzymes, kelp, barley green; borage, flax, & fish oils; Abana or Coleus forskohlii (Ayurvedic mixes), cayenne, hawthorn, fennel*
hyperactivity	*no sugar or food additives, use lecithin, chromium, calcium, magnesium, B-3, B-6, pantothenate, GABA, glutamine, valerian, kava, mineral detoxification*
hypoglycemia	*chromium, B-3, B complex, pantothenate, calcium, magnesium, low sugar diet, avoid alcohol, use small frequent meals, flax or fish oil, tryptophan, thyroid check, hyssop, red clover*
hypothyroid	*(if morning temperature less than 97.8 degrees F) kelp, iodine, tyrosine, thyroid glandular, B complex,*

FOR THIS DISORDER	USE THESE NUTRITIONAL & HERBAL HEALERS
	brewer's yeast, bladderwrack, bayberry, black cohosh, goldenseal
immune suppression	(frequent infections): diet low in sugar & fat; use A, B-complex, B-6, B-12, C, D, E, beta-carotene, CoQ, DMG; fish, flax, borage, & primrose oils; zinc, copper, germanium, iodine, iron, magnesium, manganese, selenium, mineral detoxification, arginine, glutamine, taurine, aloe, astragalus, echinacea, garlic, shiitake or maitake, ginseng, silymarin, Shosaikoto,
impotence	(also see heart disease) arginine, saw palmetto, E, C, A, beta-carotene, zinc, chromium, magnesium, liver extract, ginseng, ginkgo, Muira puama (Brazil herb), gotu kola, yohimbine; no alcohol
indigestion	aloe, betaine HCl, enzymes, Lactobacillus, psyllium, papaya, B-complex, lecithin, catnip, chamomile, comfrey, goldenseal, fennel, mint tea
infertility	avoid alcohol & caffeine, see hypothyroid; use E, A, C, B-6, B-12, folacin, enzymes, iron, selenium, zinc, liver extract, wheat germ oil, pumpkin seeds, angelica, milk thistle, for women topical progesterone (ProGest ph. 800-648-8211), for men arginine
inflammation	C & bioflavonoids, enzymes on empty stomach, zinc, selenium,

FOR THIS DISORDER	USE THESE NUTRITIONAL & HERBAL HEALERS
	magnesium, potassium, curcumin, devil's claw, feverfew, licorice, onion & garlic, Shosaikoto (Chinese herb mix), echinacea, goldenseal, pau d'arco, red clover, yucca, bilberry, topical DMSO
insomnia	*tryptophan, melatonin, calcium, magnesium, B-complex, GABA, passion flower, Suanzaorentang (Chinese herb mix), valerian, kava, catnip, hops, lady slipper, passion flower, skullcap*
irritable bowel syndrome	*diet low in fat & sugar & high in fiber, allergy detection (esp. dairy), Lactobacillus, peppermint oil (enterically coated, between meals), psyllium*
kidney & bladder problems	*lots of purified water, diet low in fat, sugar, & meat protein; cranberry extract, no alcohol or caffeine, Lactobacillus & yogurt, A, B-6, C, potassium, magnesium, glutamic acid, lysine, Desmodium styracifolium (Chinese herb mix), rose hips tea, dandelion root, pumpkin extract, goldenrod, juniper, nettle*
lead or mercury poisoning	*chelated calcium & magnesium, selenium, garlic, C & bioflavonoids (quercetin, rutin, proanthocyanidins), cysteine, NAC, glutathione, methionine, high legume diet, lots of purified water*
macular degeneration	*(including retinopathy, retinitis pigmentosa): A, C & bioflavonoids (proanthocyanidins, pycnogenol), E,*

FOR THIS DISORDER	USE THESE NUTRITIONAL & HERBAL HEALERS
	B-2, zinc, copper, manganese, selenium, taurine, bilberry, ginkgo
manic-depressive	(bipolar): tyrosine, taurine, C, B-3, B-6, B-complex, protein, zinc, calcium, magnesium, multi-vitamin & mineral; flax, borage, or fish oil; St. John's wort, kava, valerian
memory improvement	(see also heart disease) ginkgo, choline, lecithin, B-3, B-6, pantothenate, C, A, CoQ, RNA, DNA, chromium, ginseng, blue cohosh, bee pollen
meningitis	garlic, C, bioflavonoids, E, A emulsion, zinc, thymus, ginseng, echinacea, goldenseal, licorice, astragalus, catnip
menopause problems	E, topical progesterone (ProGest ph.800-648-8211), C & bioflavonoids, calcium, magnesium, B-6, lecithin; borage, primrose, flax & fish oils; phytoestrogens (soy, fennel, celery, parsley, flax, nuts), rice bran (gamma-oryzanol), tryptophan, ginseng, black cohosh, damiana, gotu kola, licorice, dong quai, raspberry
menorrhagia	(heavy menstruation): A, iron, manganese, C & bioflavonoids
migraine	B-3, rutin, multi-vitamin mineral, chromium, topical progesterone for women (ProGest ph 800-648-8211); borage, flax & fish oils; pantothen-

FOR THIS DISORDER	USE THESE NUTRITIONAL & HERBAL HEALERS
	ate, royal bee jelly, alfalfa, feverfew, ginkgo, mint
motion sickness	*ginger, magnesium, charcoal tablets, ginkgo, ginseng*
multiple sclerosis	*allergy detection, C, E, A, beta-carotene, multi-vitamin mineral, D, B-3, B-6, B-12, low fat diet, detoxification (i.e. mercury fillings), D-phenylalanine, tryptophan, kelp, Lactobacillus, calcium, magnesium, selenium, zinc, enzymes; fish, flax, borage & primrose oils; thymus, lecithin, CoQ, alfalfa, brewer's yeast*
mumps	*Lactobacillus, C, E, zinc lozenges, arginine, A from fish oil, kelp, licorice, echinacea, goldenseal, pau d'arco*
muscle cramps	*(see also hypoglycemia) calcium, magnesium, potassium, sodium, E, C, B-2, B-3, B-6, B-12, CoQ, bone meal, ginkgo, dong quai, elderberry, alfalfa, brewer's yeast, kelp*
myopathy	*(muscle disease): B-2, A, B-6, C, K, E, magnesium, selenium, carnitine, CoQ, lecithin*
nail problems	*free form amino acids, high protein diet, A, E, C, D, B-6, zinc, chromium, calcium, magnesium, lots of purified water, lecithin, flax or fish oils, kelp, thyroid check*

FOR THIS DISORDER	USE THESE NUTRITIONAL & HERBAL HEALERS
neuropathy	*(nerve problems): folacin, B-1, B-3, B-6, B-12, E, zinc, CoQ; flax or fish oils; bilberry, ginkgo, topical capsaicin*
nosebleeds	*allergy detection, detoxification (i.e.mercury fillings), no dairy; lots of purified water, alfalfa, kale, spinach, K, non-dairy acidophilus, humidifier, ginseng, licorice*
obesity	*low fat diet, exercise, chromium, carnitine, glucomannan, hydroxy-citric acid (HCA), psyllium, guar gum, xanthum gum, hyssop, lecithin, kelp, thyroid check, C, D, E, B-3, B-6, B-12 sub-lingual, CoQ, zinc, calcium, magnesium, potassium; flax, fish, borage & primrose oils; green tea, vinegar, small frequent meals, glutamine, tryptophan, xylitol, arginine & ornithine at bedtime on empty stomach*
osteoporosis	*calcium, magnesium, boron, zinc, iron, manganese, germanium, K, C, D, folacin, B-6, B-12 sub-lingual, exercise, moderate protein intake; no alcohol, caffeine, or added phosphorus (in processed foods); fish or flax oil, Lactobacillus & yogurt, topical progesterone (ProGest ph.800-648-8211)*
pain	*B-1, B-6, B-12, C, E, K, germanium, selenium, D-phenylalanine, tryptophan; topical use of cayenne, curcumin, or ginger*

FOR THIS DISORDER	USE THESE NUTRITIONAL & HERBAL HEALERS
Parkinson's	*low protein diet; use choline, lecithin, GABA, glutamic acid, D-phenylalanine, tryptophan, tyrosine, octacosanol, calcium, magnesium, zinc, chromium, folacin, B-1, B-3, B-6, B-12 sub-lingual, B-complex, C & bioflavonoids, E, selenium, brewer's yeast; primrose or borage oils*
periodontal disease	*no sugar; use CoQ, C & bioflavonoids (rutin & proantho-cyanidins), folacin, B-6, A, D, K, oral & topical E, B-complex, calcium, magnesium, zinc; toothpaste containing goldenseal, licorice, bloodroot, and zinc chloride*
pneumonia	*A from fish oil, C & bioflavonoids, E, beta-carotene, CoQ, arginine, Lactobacillus, thymus, zinc lozenges, ginger, echinacea, licorice, goldenseal, astragalus*
poison ivy	*C & bioflavonoids (quercetin), zinc, bloodroot, echinacea, goldenseal, lobelia, myrrh, Solomon's seal, poultice of white oak bark, oral & topical enzymes, oral & topical E*
pregnancy problems	*IN GENERAL: avoid alcohol & caffeine, use multi-vitamin mineral, adequate protein, folacin, B-1, B-2, B-3, B-6, A, C & bioflavonoids, E, K, calcium, magnesium, potassium, zinc, chromium, iron; flax, fish, borage & primrose oils; FOR BLEEDING GUMS: C, rutin, citrus fruit, bilberry, CoQ; FOR CONSTIPATION:*

FOR THIS DISORDER	USE THESE NUTRITIONAL & HERBAL HEALERS
	psyllium at bedtime, lots of purified water, exercise; FOR HEARTBURN: spoonful of buttermilk before eating meal, avoid spicy & greasy foods, licorice; FOR INSOMNIA: B-complex, honey & lemon tea before bed, chamomile, marjoram, lemon balm; FOR NAUSEA: small frequent meals, eat crackers upon arising, B-6, magnesium, ginger, red raspberry, basil, peppermint; FOR STRETCH MARKS: topical use of olive oil, aloe, E & A; FOR SWELLING (edema): protein (add 1 cup cottage cheese daily), B-6, magnesium, calcium, potassium
premenstrual syndrome	*avoid salt, caffeine, alcohol, sugar; use topical progesterone (ProGest ph.800-648-8211), B-6, magnesium, calcium, chromium, zinc, A, E, potassium, B-12 sub-lingual, lecithin, tyrosine, glutamine; flax, fish, borage, & primrose oils*
prostate problems	*saw palmetto, Pygeum africanum (African evergreen), pumpkin seed oil, pollen extract, A, E, C, magnesium, potassium, selenium, zinc, glutamic acid, alanine, glycine; fish, flax, primrose & borage oils; decoction of gravel root, sea holly, and hydrangea*
psoriasis	*flax or fish oils, oral & topical D, A, E, folacin, B-12, chromium, selenium, zinc, brewer's yeast, kelp, lecithin, undecylenic acid, silymarin; poultice of dandelion, sarsaparilla,*

FOR THIS DISORDER	USE THESE NUTRITIONAL & HERBAL HEALERS
	yellow dock & lavender; topical capsaicin or Oleum Horwathiensis (Hungary herb mix)
Raynaud's	*B-3, E, magnesium; borage, primrose, fish & flax oils*
restless legs	*avoid caffeine & sugar; use folacin, E, iron, tryptophan*
schizophrenia	*extra protein, tyrosine, glutamine, lecithin, C, CoQ, ginkgo, B-complex, B-3, B-6, zinc, chromium, flax, fish, primrose & borage oils*
seborrhea	*primrose, borage, flax & fish oils; A, zinc, selenium, biotin, B-6 ointment, B-12 sub-lingual, B-complex, E, CoQ, lecithin, dandelion, goldenseal Vitastic lotion (Alacer, 800-854-0249)*
senility	*(see heart disease) protein, glutamine, lecithin, tyrosine, B-complex, B-3, B-12 sub-lingual, folacin, CoQ, zinc, chromium, ginkgo, blue cohosh, anise*
shingles	*(herpes zoster) cayenne oral & topical (as Zostrix), C & bioflavonoids, lysine, B-12, B-complex, zinc, A, D, E, CoQ, bovine cartilage, echinacea, goldenseal, licorice, astragalus*
sinusitis	*allergy detection, avoid dairy, smoke, dust, & fumes; use bee pollen, garlic, zinc, warm salt water nasal purge, B-6, B-complex, echinacea, C & bioflavonoids*

FOR THIS DISORDER	USE THESE NUTRITIONAL & HERBAL HEALERS
smoking cessation	B-complex, B-1, lobelia, glutamine, C, E, beta-carotene, selenium, chromium, brewer's yeast, kava, valerian, hops
tonsillitis	C & bioflavonoids, E, A, beta-carotene, D, B-6, B-complex, allergy detection, Lactobacillus, fish or flax oils, echinacea, pau d'arco, sage, licorice, goldenseal, chamomile
ulcer (duodenal & gastric)	avoid alcohol, caffeine, tea, milk, sugar; use aloe, licorice, A, E, B-6, C & bioflavonoids (catechin), calcium, magnesium, zinc, bismuth, S-methylmethionine, glutamine; high fiber diet plus pectin & psyllium; flax or fish oil, zinc, bilberry, chamomile, goldenseal root, rhubarb, myrrh, sage, slippery elm, cayenne
ulcer (skin)	folacin, oral & topical A, C, E, selenium, zinc, hydroxyethylrutosides, primrose oil; topical lotion of free form amino acids, C, & white sugar
underweight/poor appetite	(see hypothyroid), enzymes, liver extract, B-complex, folacin, B-6, zinc, magnesium, protein, fenugreek, catnip
urticaria (skin eruptions)	allergy detection, beta-carotene, B-3, B-12, C, magnesium
vaginitis	Lactobacillus (oral & douche), garlic, flax or fish oils, A, E, C, D, calcium, magnesium

FOR THIS DISORDER	USE THESE NUTRITIONAL & HERBAL HEALERS
varicose veins	C & bioflavonoids (rutin, hesperidin, proanthocyanidins), ginkgo, B-3, E, chromium, zinc, lecithin, potassium
vertigo (dizziness)	ginger, ginkgo
wound healing	diet high in protein & low in fat, pantothenate, B-1, oral & topical A, E, C & bioflavonoids (proanthocyanidins), copper, manganese, oral & topical zinc, enzymes, glutathione, arginine; fish, flax, borage & primrose oils; gotu kola; topical use of glycosaminoglycans, aloe, sugar, chamomile, echinacea, or tea tree oil
worms/parasites	cloves, wormwood, wormseed, black walnut, iodine, garlic, C, pumpkin extract, male fern, pinkroot

Personal Profile

While I have learned a great deal from patients that recover with my guidance, I learn just as much from failures. Here is just one example. GB was a bright and caring 42 year old male with cancer of the larynx, the voice box. His physician in his home town had surgically removed the larynx, so that GB now had to talk through an amplified electronic pipe. In spite of this surgery, the cancer had spread throughout his body and was threatening his life. He was interested in taking whatever nutritional supplements might help him beat this awful disease.

As I worked with GB, I asked him some questions about his personal life. I have found that about 90% of the hundreds of cancer patients that I have worked with have experienced some major stressful incident a year or two prior to the onset of the cancer. The resulting mental depression leads to a depressed immune system, which then allows cancer to take over. GB mentioned that a year before finding out about his cancer, his wife had left him. He wanted to continue the marriage and tried to stop her from leaving, to which she commented: "there's nothing you can say that will make me stay." He could say nothing to save his marriage. The cancer settled in to his voice box.

He was treated with chemotherapy, radiation and substantial amounts of nutrition factors to slow his cancer--all to no avail. The hurt from his failed marriage probably allowed the cancer to spread through his body like a fire through a dry forest.

Vitamin C will not cure a broken heart. Garlic will not give you a reason to live. Fish oil will not ease the pain of loneliness. If our physical problems begins in the emotional and spiritual arena, as it did for GB, then that is where the cure will be found. For recovery from life threatening diseases, it is absolutely crucial to get your mind free from hurt, anger, rage, depression, and low self-esteem.

CHAPTER 5

◆

HEALTH BENEFITS FROM GOD'S KITCHEN

Joshua1:8 *Do not let this Book of the Law depart from your mouth; meditate on it day and night, so that you may be careful to do everything written in it. Then you will be prosperous and successful.*

Personal Profile

MW was a widower who had developed bad eating habits since his wife died a year ago. He had just come down with the agonizingly painful "shingles", or the virus herpes zoster, when he came to see me. I asked him to re-think the concept of eating properly. He admitted that he had many reasons to be thankful and continue living, especially for his church groups and grandchildren. I told him about bulk cooking--spending 2 hours each week in the kitchen to make sure that you have healthy food for the rest of the week. I also put him on a broad spectrum vitamin and mineral supplement, plus extra vitamin C, E, fish oil, lecithin, magnesium, chromium, zinc, and the herb for improving circulation, ginkgo. Those would help him in the near future. But for right now, he needed immediate relief from the pain of his shingles. I asked him to take 9 grams daily of bovine tracheal cartilage. His shingles cleared up within 3 days. After 2 months, he commented on a better memory and more energy.

*F*or the first 5000 years of civilization, humans relied on foods and herbs for medicine. Only in the past 50 years have we forgotten our medicinal "roots" in favor of patent medicines. While prescription pharmaceuticals have their value, there are many well-documented, non-toxic and inexpensive healing properties in whole foods. The following list is but a sampling of the health benefits from God's wholesome foods. For more information see:

† *THE HEALING POWER OF FOODS* by Dr. Michael Murray
† *FOOD: YOUR MIRACLE MEDICINE* by Jean Carper
† *HEALING FOODS* by Patti Hausman, MS
† *HEINERMAN'S ENCYCLOPEDIA OF FRUITS, VEGETABLES, AND HERBS,* by John Heinerman
† *FOODS THAT HEAL*, by Maureen Salaman

Apple. Lowers cholesterol and risk for cancer. Has mild antibacterial, antiviral, anti-inflammatory, estrogenic activity. High in fiber, helps avoid constipation, suppresses appetite. Juice can cause diarrhea in children.

Asparagus. A super source of the antioxidant, glutathione, to lower cancer risk.

Avocado. Benefits circulation, lowers cholesterol, dilates blood vessels. Its main fat, monounsaturated oleic acid (also concentrated in olive oil), acts as an antioxidant to block artery-destroying toxicity of bad-type LDL cholesterol. One of the richest sources of glutathione, a powerful antioxidant, shown to block thirty different carcinogens and to block proliferation of the AIDS virus in test tube experiments.

Banana and **Plantain**. Soothes the stomach. Good for dyspepsia (upset stomach). Strengthens the stomach lining against acid and ulcers. Has antibiotic activity.

Barley. Long known as a "heart medicine" in the Middle East. Reduces cholesterol. Has antiviral and anticancer activity. Contains potent antioxidants, including tocotrienols.

Beans (legumes, including navy, black, kidney, pinto, soy beans and lentils). Potent medicine in lowering cholesterol. One-half cup of cooked beans daily reduces cholesterol an average 10 percent. Regulates blood sugar levels. An excellent food for diabetics. Linked to lower rates of certain cancers. Very high in fiber. A leading producer of intestinal gas in most people. Gas can be reduced through the following method: bring beans to a boil for 2 minutes, turn off stove burner and let beans sit in water for 1 hour, discard this water, then pressure cook beans for about 30 minutes, depending on which bean you are cooking.

Bell Pepper. Rich in antioxidant vitamin C. Helps to fight off colds, asthma, bronchitis, respiratory infections, cataracts, macular degeneration, angina, atherosclerosis and cancer.

Blueberry. Acts as an unusual type antibiotic by blocking attachment of bacteria that cause urinary tract infections. Contains chemicals that curb diarrhea. Also antiviral activity and high in natural aspirin.

Broccoli. A unique package of versatile disease-fighters. Abundant in antioxidants, including quercetin, glutathione, beta carotene, indoles, vitamin C, lutein, glucarate, sulforaphane. Extremely high anti-cancer activity, particularly against lung, colon and breast cancers. Like other cruciferous vegetables, it speeds up removal of estrogen from the body, helping suppress breast cancer. Rich in cholesterol-reducing fiber. Has antiviral, anti-ulcer activity. A super source of chromium that helps regulate insulin and blood sugar. Note: cooking and processing destroys some of the antioxidants and antiestrogenic agents, such as indoles and glutathione. Most protective when eaten raw or lightly cooked, as in microwaving.

Brussels Sprouts. Cruciferous family possesses some of the same powers as broccoli and cabbage. Definitely anti-cancer, anti-estrogenic and packed with various antioxidants and indoles.

Cabbage (including bok choy). Revered in ancient Rome as a cancer cure. Contains numerous anticancer and antioxidant compounds. Speeds up estrogen metabolism, is thought to help block breast cancer and suppress growth of polyps, a prelude to colon cancer. Eating cabbage more than once a week cut men's colon cancer odds 66 percent. As little as two daily tablespoons of cooked cabbage protected against stomach cancer. Contains anti-ulcer compounds; cabbage juice helps heal ulcers in humans. Has antibacterial and anti-viral powers. Can cause flatulence in some. Some of these important compounds are destroyed by cooking. Raw cabbage, as in cole slaw, appears to have stronger overall health value.

Carrot. A super source of beta carotene, a powerful anticancer, artery-protecting, immune-boosting, infection-fighting antioxidant with wide protective powers. A carrot a day slashed stroke rates in women by 68 percent. One medium carrot's worth of beta carotene cuts lung cancer risk in half, even among formerly heavy smokers. High doses of beta carotene, as found in carrots, substantially reduces odds of degenerative eye diseases (cataracts and macular degeneration) as well as chest pain (angina). Carrots' high soluble fiber depresses blood cholesterol, promotes regularity. Cooking can make it easier for the body to absorb beta carotene.

Cauliflower. Cruciferous family member that contains many of the same cancer-fighting, hormone-regulating compounds as its cousins, broccoli and cabbage. Specifically thought to help ward off breast and colon cancers. Eat raw, lightly cooked or microwaved.

Celery. A traditional Vietnamese remedy for high blood pressure. Celery compounds reduce blood pressure in animals. Comparable human dose: two to four stalks a day. Also has a mild diuretic effect. Contains eight different families of anticancer compounds, such as phthalides and polyacetylenes, that detoxify carcinogens, especially cigarette smoke. Eating celery before or after vigorous exercise can induce mild to serious allergic reactions in some.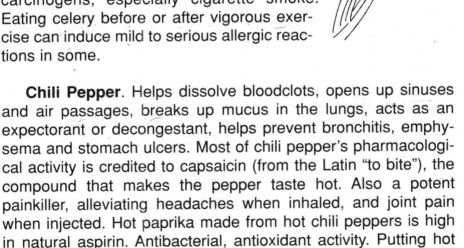

Chili Pepper. Helps dissolve bloodclots, opens up sinuses and air passages, breaks up mucus in the lungs, acts as an expectorant or decongestant, helps prevent bronchitis, emphysema and stomach ulcers. Most of chili pepper's pharmacological activity is credited to capsaicin (from the Latin "to bite"), the compound that makes the pepper taste hot. Also a potent painkiller, alleviating headaches when inhaled, and joint pain when injected. Hot paprika made from hot chili peppers is high in natural aspirin. Antibacterial, antioxidant activity. Putting hot chili sauce on food also speeds up metabolism, burning off calories. Chili peppers do not harm the stomach lining or promote ulcers.

Chocolate. Contains chemicals thought to affect neurotransmitters in the brain. Added to milk, chocolate helps counteract lactose intolerance. Chocolate does not seem to raise choles-terol. Dark chocolate is high in copper, which may help ward off cardiovascular disease. Triggers headaches in some. Aggravates heartburn. Implicated in cystic breast disease.

Cinnamon. A strong stimulator of insulin activity, thus poten-tially helpful for those with Type II diabetes. Mild anticoagulant activity.

Clove. Used to kill the pain of toothache and as an anti-inflammatory against rheumatic diseases. Has anticoagulant effects, (anti-platelet aggregation), and its main ingredient, eugenol, is anti-inflammatory.

Coffee. Most, but not all, of coffee's pharma-cological impact comes from its high con-centration of caffeine, a psychoactive drug. Caffeine, depending on an individual's biological makeup and peculiar sensitivity, can be a mood elevator and mental energizer. Improves mental performance in some. An emergency remedy for asthma. Dilates bronchial passages. Mildly addictive. Triggers headaches, anxi-ety and panic attacks in some. In excess may cause psychiatric disturbances. Promotes insomnia. Coffee stimulates stomach acid secretion (both caffeinated and decaf). Can aggravate heartburn. Promotes bowel movements in many, causes diar-rhea in others. Caffeine may promote fibrocystic breast disease in some women.

Collard Greens, Full of anticancer, antioxidant compounds, including lutein, vitamin C, beta carotene. In animals blocks the spread of breast cancer. Like other green leafy vegetables, associated with low rates of all cancers.

Corn Anticancer and antiviral activity, possibly induced by corn's content of protease inhibitors. Has estrogen-boosting capabilities. A very common cause of food intolerance linked to symptoms of rheumatoid arthritis, irritable bowel syndrome, headaches and migraine-related epilepsy in children.

Cranberry. Strong antibiotic properties with unusual abilities to prevent infectious bacteria from sticking to cells lining the bladder and urinary tract. Thus, it helps prevent recurring urinary tract (bladder) infections. Also has antiviral activity.

Date. High in natural aspirin. Has laxative effect. Dried fruits, including dates, are linked to lower rates of certain cancers, especially pancreatic cancer. Contains compounds that may cause headaches in susceptible individuals.

Eggplant. Eggplant substances called glycoalkaloids, made into a topical cream medication, have been used to treat skin cancers such as basal cell carcinoma, according to Australian researchers. Also, eating eggplant may lower blood cholesterol and help counteract some detrimental blood effects of fatty foods. Eggplant also has antibacterial and diuretic properties.

Fenugreek Seeds. A spice common in the Middle East and available in many U.S. food markets. Has anti-diabetic powers. Helps control surges of blood sugar and insulin. Also anti-diarrheal, anti-ulcer, anti-cancer, tends to lower blood pressure, helps prevent intestinal gas.

Fig. Helps to prevent cancer. Both extract of figs and the fig compound benzaldehyde have helped shrink tumors in humans, according to Japanese tests. Also laxative, anti-ulcer, anti-bacterial and anti-parasitic powers. Triggers headaches in some people.

Fish and Fish Oil. An ounce a day has been shown to cut risk of heart attacks 50 percent. Oil in fish can relieve symptoms of rheumatoid arthritis, osteoarthritis, asthma, psoriasis, high blood pressure, Raynaud's disease, migraine headaches, ulcerative colitis, possibly multiple sclerosis. May help ward off strokes. A known anti-inflammatory agent and anticoagulant. Raises good type HDL cholesterol. Lowers triglycerides. Guards against glucose intolerance and Type II diabetes. Some fish are high in antioxidants, such as selenium and Coenzyme Q-10. Exhibits anticancer activity especially in blocking development of colon cancer and spread of breast cancer. Fish highest in omega-3 fatty acids include sardines, mackerel, herring, salmon, tuna.

Garlic. Used to treat an array of ills since the dawn of civilization. Broad-spectrum antibiotic that combats bacteria, intestinal parasites and viruses. In high doses it has cured encephalitis. Lowers blood pressure and blood cholesterol, discourages dangerous blood clotting. Two or three cloves a day cut the odds of subsequent heart attacks in half in heart patients. Contains multiple anticancer compounds and antioxidants and tops the National Cancer Institute's list as a potential cancer-preventive food. Lessens chances of stomach cancer in particular. A good cold medication. Acts as a decongestant, expectorant, anti-spasmodic, anti-inflammatory agent. Boosts immune responses. Helps relieve gas, has antidiarrheal, estrogenic and diuretic activity. Appears to lift mood and has a mild calming effect. High doses of raw garlic (more than three cloves a day) have caused gas, bloating, diarrhea and fever in some. Aged garlic may be better than cooked garlic. Eat garlic both raw and cooked for all-around insurance.

Ginger. Used to treat nausea, vomiting, headaches, chest congestion, cholera, colds, diarrhea, stomach ache, rheumatism, and nervous diseases. Ginger is a proven anti-nausea, anti-motion sickness remedy that matches or surpasses drugs such as Dramamine. Helps thwart and prevent migraine headaches and osteoarthritis. Relieves symptoms of rheumatoid arthritis. Acts as an anti-thrombotic and anti-inflammatory agent in humans; is an antibiotic in test tubes (kills salmonella and staph bacteria), and an anti-ulcer agent in animals. Also, has anti-depressant, anti-diarrheal and strong antioxidant activity. High in anti-cancer activity.

Grape. Rich in antioxidant compounds. Red grapes (but not white or green grapes), are high in antioxidant quercetin. Grape skins contain resveratrol, shown to inhibit blood-platelet clumping (and consequently, blood clot formation) and boost good-type HDL cholesterol. Red grapes are antibacterial and antiviral in test tubes. Grapeseed oil also raises good-type HDL cholesterol.

Grapefruit. The pulp contains a unique pectin (in membranes and juice sacs—not in juice) that lowers blood cholesterol and reverses atherosclerosis (clogged arteries) in animals. Has anticancer activity, and appears particularly protective against stomach and pancreatic cancer. The juice is antiviral. High in various antioxidants, especially vitamin C.

Honey. Strong antibiotic properties. Has sleep-inducing sedative and tranquilizing properties.

Kale. Rich source of various anticancer chemicals. Has more beta carotene than spinach and twice as much lutein, the most of any vegetable tested. Kale is also a member of the cruciferous family, endowing it with anticancer indoles that help regulate estrogen and fight off colon cancer.

Kiwi Fruit. Commonly prescribed in Chinese traditional medicine to treat stomach and breast cancer. Rich in digestive enzymes. High in vitamin C.

Licorice. Strong anticancer powers, possibly because of a high concentration of glycyrrhizin. Mice drinking glycyrrhizin dissolved in water have fewer skin cancers. Also kills bacteria, fights ulcers and diarrhea. May act as a diuretic. Too much licorice can raise blood pressure. Also it is not advised for pregnant women. Only real licorice has these powers. "Licorice" candy sold in the United States is made with anise instead of real licorice. Real licorice says "licorice mass." Imitation licorice is labeled "artificial licorice" or "anise."

Melon (green and yellow, such as cantaloupe and honeydew). Has anticoagulant (blood-thinning) activity. Contains antioxidant beta carotene.

Milk. Cancer-fighting powers, possibly against colon, lung, stomach and cervical cancers, especially in low-fat milk. One study detected less cancer among low-fat milk drinkers than non-milk drinkers. May help prevent high blood pressure. Skim milk may lower blood cholesterol. Milk fat promotes cancer and heart disease. Milk is also an unappreciated terror in triggering "allergic" reactions that induce joint pain and symptoms of rheumatoid arthritis, asthma, irritable bowel syndrome and diarrhea. In children and infants, milk is suspected to cause or contribute to colic, respiratory problems, sleeplessness, itchy rashes, migraines, epileptic seizures, ear infections and even diabetes. May retard healing of ulcers.

Mushroom (including maitake & shiitake; grow on rotting wood stumps). A longevity tonic, heart medicine and cancer remedy in Asia. Current tests show mushrooms, such as maitake, help prevent and/or treat cancer, viral diseases, such as influenza and polio, high blood cholesterol, sticky blood

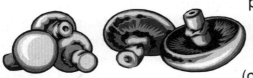

platelets and high blood pressure. Eaten daily, maitake or shiitake, fresh (three ounces) or dried (one-third ounce) cut cholesterol by 7 and 12 percent respectively. A shiitake compound, lentinan, is a broad-spectrum antiviral agent that potentiates immune functioning. Used to treat leukemia in China and breast cancer in Japan. Extract (sulfated B-glucans) has been declared by Japanese scientists more effective as an AIDS drug than the common drug AZT. Eating black ("tree ear") mushroom "thins the blood." No therapeutic effects are known for the common U.S. button mushroom. Some claim this species has cancer-causing potential (hydrazides) unless cooked.

Mustard (including horseradish). Recognized for centuries as a decongestant and expectorant. Helps break up mucus in air passages. A good remedy for congestion caused by colds and sinus problems. Also antibacterial. Increases metabolism, burning off extra calories. In one British test about three-fifths of a teaspoon of ordinary yellow mustard increased metabolic rate about 25 percent, burning forty-five more calories in three hours.

Nuts. Anticancer and heart-protective properties. A key food among Seventh-Day Adventists, known for their low rates of heart disease. Walnuts and almonds help reduce cholesterol, contain high concentrations of antioxidant oleic acid and monounsaturated fat, similar to that in olive oil, known to protect arteries from damage. Nuts generally are high in antioxidant vitamin E, shown to protect against chest pain and artery damage. Brazil nuts are extremely rich in selenium, an antioxidant linked to lower rates of heart disease and cancer. Walnuts contain ellagic acid, an antioxidant and cancer-fighter, and are also high in omega-3 type oil. Nuts, including peanuts, are good regulators of insulin and blood sugar, preventing steep rises, making them good foods for those with glucose intolerance and diabetes. Peanuts also are estrogenic. Nuts have been found lacking in the diets of those who later develop Parkinson's disease. Prime cause of acute allergic reactions in susceptible individuals.

Oats. Can depress cholesterol 10 percent or more, depending on individual responses. Oats help stabilize blood sugar, have estrogenic and antioxidant activity. They also contain psychoactive compounds that may combat nicotine cravings and have antidepressant powers. High doses can cause gas, abdominal bloating and pain in some.

Olive oil. Lowers bad LDL cholesterol without lowering good HDL cholesterol. Helps keep bad cholesterol from being converted to a toxic or "oxidized" form. Thus, helps protect arteries from plaque. Reduces blood pressure, helps regulate blood sugar. Has potent antioxidant activity. Best oil for kitchen cooking and salads.

Onion (including chives, shallots, scallions, leeks). Reputed in ancient Mesopotamia to cure virtually everything. An exceptionally strong antioxidant. Full of numerous anticancer agents. Blocks cancer dramatically in animals. The onion is the richest dietary source of quercetin, a potent antioxidant (in shallots, yellow and red onions only—not white onions). Specifically linked to inhibiting human stomach cancer. Thins the blood, lowers cholesterol, raises good-type HDL cholesterol (preferred dose: half a raw onion a day), wards off blood clots, fights asthma, chronic bronchitis, hay fever, diabetes, atherosclerosis and infections. Anti-inflammatory, antibiotic, antiviral, thought to have diverse anticancer powers. Quercetin is also a sedative. Onions aggravate heartburn, may promote gas.

Orange. Natural cancer-inhibitor, includes carotenoids, terpenes and flavonoids. Also rich in antioxidant vitamin C and beta carotene. Specifically tied to lower rates of pancreatic cancer. Orange juice protected mice sperm from radiation damage. Because of its high vitamin C, oranges may help ward off asthma attacks, bronchitis, breast cancer, stomach cancer, atherosclerosis, gum disease, and boost fertility and healthy sperm in some men. A compound in the peeling of citrus (limonene) has shown remarkable anti-cancer properties. May aggravate heartburn.

Parsley. Anticancer because of its high concentrations of antioxidants, such as monoterpenes, phthalides, polyacetylenes. Can help detoxify carcinogens and neutralize certain carcinogens in tobacco smoke. Also, has diuretic activity.

Pineapple. Suppresses inflammation. A main constituent, an antibacterial enzyme called bromelain, is anti-inflammatory. Pineapple aids digestion, helps dissolve blood clots and is good for preventing osteoporosis and bone fractures because of its very high manganese content. It is also antibacterial and antiviral and mildly estrogenic.

Plum. Antibacterial. Antiviral. Laxative.

Potato (white). Contains anticancer protease inhibitors. High in potassium, thus may help prevent high blood pressure and strokes. Contains a compound, gamma-amino butyric acid (GABA) that may have sedative activity. Some estrogenic activity.

Prune. A well-known laxative. High in fiber, sorbitol and natural aspirin.

Pumpkin. Extremely high in beta carotene, the antioxidant reputed to help ward off numerous health problems, including heart attacks, cancer, cataracts.

Raspberry. Antiviral, anticancer activity. High in natural aspirin.

Rice. Antidiarrheal, anticancer activity. Like other seeds, contains anticancer protease inhibitors. Of all grains and cereals, it is the least likely to provoke intestinal gas or adverse reactions (intolerances), causing bowel distress such as spastic colon. Rice bran is excellent against constipation, lowers cholesterol and tends to block development of kidney stones.

Seaweed and **Kelp**. Antibacterial and antiviral activity in brown Laminaria type seaweed known as kelp. It kills herpes virus, for example. Kelp may also lower blood pressure and cholesterol. Wakame boosts immune functioning. Nori kills bacteria and seems to help heal ulcers. A chemical from wakame seaweed is a clot-buster, in one test twice as powerful as the common drug heparin. Most types of seaweed have anticancer activity. Might aggravate acne flare-ups.

Soybean. Rich in hormones, it boosts estrogen levels in postmenopausal women. Has anticancer activity and is thought to be especially antagonistic to breast cancer, possibly one reason rates of breast and prostate cancers are low among the Japanese. Soybeans are the richest source of potent protease inhibitors which are anticancer, antiviral agents. Soybeans lower blood cholesterol substantially. In animals, soybeans seem to deter and help dissolve kidney stones.

Spinach. Tops the list, along with other green leafy vegetables, as a food most eaten by people who don't get cancer. A super source of antioxidants and cancer antagonists, containing about four times more beta carotene and three times more lutein than broccoli, for example. Rich in fiber that helps lower blood cholesterol. Some of its antioxidants are destroyed by cooking. Eat raw or lightly cooked.

Strawberry. Antiviral, anticancer activity. Often eaten by people less likely to develop all types of cancer.

Sugar. Helps heal wounds when applied externally. Like other carbohydrates, sugar helps induce cavities. Also may be related to Crohn's disease. Triggers rises in blood sugar and stimulates insulin production. Taken orally, refined white sugar is more of a drug than a food.

Sweet Potato (yams). A source of the antioxidant beta carotene, linked to preventing heart disease, cataracts, strokes and numerous cancers. One half cup of mashed sweet potatoes contains about 14 milligrams of beta carotene, or about 23,000 international units (IUs).

Tea (including black, oolong and green tea, not herbal teas). Amazing and diverse pharmacological activity, mainly due to catechins. Tea acts as an anticoagulant, artery protector, antibiotic, anti-ulcer agent, cavity-fighter, antidiarrheal agent, antiviral agent, diuretic (caffeine), analgesic (caffeine), mild sedative (decaffeinated). In animals tea and tea compounds are potent blockers of various cancers. Tea drinkers appear to have less atherosclerosis (damaged, clogged arteries) and fewer strokes. Excessive tea drinking, because of its caffeine, could aggravate anxiety, insomnia and symptoms of PMS. Tea may also promote kidney stones because of its high oxalate content. Green tea, popular in Asian countries, is highest in catechins, followed by oolong and ordinary black tea, common in the United States.

Green tea is considered most potent. One human study, however, found no difference in benefits to arteries from green or black tea.

Tomato. A major source of lycopene, an antioxidant and anticancer agent that intervenes in devastating chain reactions of oxygen free radical molecules. Tomatoes are linked in particular to lower rates of pancreatic cancer and cervical cancer.

Turmeric. Truly one of the marvelous medicinal spices of the world. Its main active ingredient is curcumin which gives turmeric its intense cadmium yellow color. Curcumin, studies show, is an anti-inflammatory agent on a par with cortisone, and has reduced inflammation in animals and symptoms of rheumatoid arthritis in humans. In other tests, it lowered cholesterol, hindered platelet aggregation (blood clotting), protected the liver from toxins, boosted stomach defenses against acid, lowered blood sugar in diabetics, and was a powerful antagonist of numerous cancer-causing agents. Anticancer activity.

Watermelon. High amounts of lycopene and glutathione, antioxidant and anticancer compounds. Also mild antibacterial, anticoagulant activity.

Wheat, High-fiber whole wheat, and particularly wheat bran, rank as the world's greatest preventives of constipation. Wheat bran can suppress cancer development in the colon. Antiparasitic. Ranks exceedingly high as a trigger of food intolerances and allergies, resulting in symptoms of rheumatoid arthritis, irritable bowel syndrome and neurological illnesses.

Yogurt. An ancient wonder food, strongly antibacterial and anticancer. A cup or two of yogurt a day boosts immune functioning by stimulating production of gamma interferon. Also spurs activity of natural killer cells that attack viruses and tumors. A daily cup of yogurt reduced colds and other upper respiratory infections in humans. Helps prevent and cure diarrhea. A daily cup of yogurt with acidophilus cultures prevents vaginitis (yeast infections) in women. Helps fight bone problems, such as osteoporosis, because of high available calcium content. Acidophilus yogurt cultures neutralize cancer-causing agents in the intestinal tract. Plain old yogurt with L. bulgaricus and S. thermophilus cultures, both live and dead, blocked lung cancers in animals. The live bacteria in yogurt helps people with lactose intolerance to digest lactose (milk sugar).

CHAPTER 6

◆

NUTRITITOUS
AND DELICIOUS
ONE WEEK MEAL PLAN WITH RECIPES

BY NOREEN QUILLIN & PATRICK QUILLIN

Personal Profile

KO and DO were a wonderful loving professional couple who had been frustrated in their attempts to have children. Several doctors told them that his sperm count was
borderline too low and that she may not have enough
progesterone to keep the fertilized egg from being reject-
ed in menstruation. Their story is far too typical.
American men are suffering from a dramatic reduction in
sperm count when compared to our ancestors. Much of
the current infertility is due to pollution, stress, and poor

diet.

KO was put on an aggressive detoxification program, involving high fiber foods, fasting one day each week, using silymarin for liver detox, selenium and vitamin E to bolster the glutathione peroxidase detox system in the body, taking herbal purgatives (Perfect 7 and Body Cleanse) at night on an empty stomach, broad spectrum vitamin and mineral supplements, vitamin C along with lots of purified water to flush out the system, and regular hot baths to cleanse the pores of the skin. He also avoided red meat and was only allowed fish or poultry twice each week. While doing this detoxification process, he also took arginine to help build sperm count. Within 3 months, his sperm count was considered "normal".

DO was found to have a low thyroid output, based on her basal temperature first thing in the morning. Though she never had endometriosis (a condition of abnormal uterus), she did have regular heavy periods. I put her on vitamin A supplements from fish oil for the heavy periods. We tried gentle natural healers to get her thyroid gland "jump started", including supplements of kelp, taking tyrosine and iodine at night on an empty stomach, and the herb bladderwrack. These efforts failed to get her morning temperature up above the required minimum of 97.8 degress Fahrenheit. Her physician then prescribed natural dessicated thyroid tablets, which did bring her morning temperature up and brought back a renewed sex drive that she thought was lost forever. She also started using progesterone lotion on her thigh at night after her ovulation time. This would help the body to retain a fertilized egg. She also began taking the helpful fertility herb angelica.

Within 6 months, they were pregnant, much healthier than before, and very happy about the prospects for their future.

This cookbook section was written with the loving assistance of my talented wife, Noreen, to provide a starting point for your new healthy lifestyle. Included are:

† tips on dining out
† drinks to emphasize
† my personal creation, the "dragon slayer" shake that I consume daily
† bulk cooking tips, such as making your own yogurt and sprouting grains
† one full week of menus along with the recipes mentioned
† simple exchanges to make in the kitchen for dramatic improvements in your nutrient intake.

This section will show you how to prepare meals that can be tasty and nutritious. The recipes are just a guide to show you the possibilities in creative cooking. See the appendix for other good cook books.

Realize that there is no one perfect diet. This chapter demonstrates healthy eating habits within the context of practical and tasty recipes. There are some noteworthy spartan diets that only an extremely dedicated person can follow. Gleaning from dozens of good cookbooks and years of experience, this menu provides precious few compromises in nutritional quality while emphasizing taste, cost and practical preparation of whole foods.

GIVE IT A CHANCE

Our eating habits are all acquired. We base our current diet on what mother cooked when we were younger; what our society, ethnic and religious groups prefer; what we see advertised, and what is available in the local grocery store. People in the Phillipines or the Amazon are born with structurally identical taste buds to Americans, yet they eat entirely different foods.

Realize that it takes about 3 weeks to acquire new eating habits. Try this program for 3 weeks, at which time it will become easier to stay with. You just might find that the nutrient-depleted junk food of yesterday really doesn't satisfy your taste buds like the following whole foods.

COMMONLY ASKED QUESTIONS:

Question. Many people are on the go and don't feel that they have time to plan healthy meals. Any suggestions?

Answer. Cook in bulk. Freeze leftovers in serving size packets. You can then make your own TV dinners. Crockpot cooking is good because the food is ready when you arrive home hungry. Have fruits and vegetables on hand. Simplify cooking by leaving out heavy sauces and creams. Put foods that cook at the same tempeture in the oven when arriving home. Plan ahead. Eat smaller portions throughout the day, then you won't be starving by dinner time and pick up fast food.

Q. Can people eat out and still eat nourishing meals?

A. Plan ahead. Beware of sauces & high fat cheese in "healthy restaurants". Read the menu. Control portions. You don't need to clean the plate. Ask for a carry home container when ordering the food and then divide the food before you start eating. Have vegetables unbuttered. Order a salad served instead of chips.

Iceberg lettuce is the most common salad bar offering, but is "junk food" relative to most other vegetables. Skip the iceberg lettuce and enjoy the healthier fruits, vegetables and whole-grain foods from the salad bar. A good rule of thumb: the deeper the color of the vegetable, the more nourishing it is. Dark greens are better than pale greens, dark orange squash is better than pale squash, and so on. In nature, cauliflower is a dark green vegetable, until human intervention ties the leaves around the developing flower to deprive it of sunlight.

Many restaurants offer low-calorie or light meals with gourmet versions. Instead of accepting that "fried" meal from a restaurant menu, most places will steam or broil your food. Airlines can be very accommodating in having a special meal ready for you. Give them at least 1 week advance notice. Ask for the salad dressing to be served on the side. Avoid: a la mode, au gratin, basted, bisque, casserole, creamed, sauteed, fried etc. Have rich sauces or gravies left out.

Q. What is the best way to cook vegetables?

A. Cook to a crisp-tender stage. Microwave. Steaming is much better than boiling. Use spices to flavor but do not overpower the vegetable..

Q. Can you cut sugar in a favorite recipe?

A. Use concentrated fruit juices, applesauce, crushed pineapple and mashed bananas instead of sugar. Cinnamon or vanilla will enhance the sweetness. If a recipe calls for 1 cup of sugar, then instead substitute with one of the following:
-1/4 to 1/3 cup honey. You must reduce the liquid in the recipe by 3 Tbs or add 3 Tbs. flour. Reduce heat by about 25 degrees
-3 mashed bananas & 1 tsp. cinnamon
-1/2 cup dried fruit puree
-1 cup unsweetened applesauce or crushed pineapple with 1 tsp. cinnamon
-1 cup apple juice plus 1/3 cup nonfat dry milk powder as substitute for 1 cup milk in recipe

Q. How can a person cut back on salt?

A. Our taste for salty foods has been acquired. Gradually cut back on the use of highly processed foods and salty snacks. Cook with herb blends instead of salt. Use more garlic, hot peppers, curry, cloves, and ginger, which are very healthy seasoning herbs. Use "Lite salt", which is made up of regular salt diluted with the helpful minerals of potassium, magnesium, and calcium in your salt shaker.

Q. Do you have a helpful suggestion if someone eats too fast?

A. Make dining a separate experience. No TV. Dine only while sitting at the dining table. Begin a meal with hot soup, or salad, or fresh fruit as an appetizer. This provides bulk. Never serve food "family style". Completely chew food to a liquid and swallow before putting more food on the fork.

Q. There are many studies on the benifits of garlic but the taste is pretty strong and bad breath would be a problem for me at work. Is there a way to prepare garlic that will "soften" the flavor?

A. Break a bulb of garlic into cloves. You don't need to peel them. Place in a coffee cup. Sprinkle on some olive oil. Add a bit of spike or your favorite low salt seasoning. Stir until the cloves have been coated. Place plastic wrap over the top. Microwave for about 45 seconds. Your garlic will peel easily and taste somewhat like spring potatoes.

Q. We all know that breakfast is important but we don't have the time in the morning to cook a big meal. What can we do to nourish ourselves?

A. Americans eat 80-85% of the day's calories in just a few concentrated hours, usually in the evening. Some people skip
breakfast because they don't feel as hungry compared to when
they eat breakfast. The reason for this unusual effect is that
when you starve in the morning, the waste products (ketones)
are released in the blood stream depressing the appetite. But as
soon as you eat, you will overeat. Some fast breakfast ideas
are: hard boiled eggs prepared in advance, protein bar, hot
instant cereals, whole grain cold cereals with apple juice for
moisture, pancakes left over from the weekend, bowl of yogurt,
a whole wheat bagel with no-fat cream cheese, mixed drink of
fruit juice with protein powder.

Q. Are there any tips to be aware of when shopping for gro-
ceries?

A. Don't shop when you're hungry. Eat a variety of foods, which
will improve nutrient intake and reduce exposure to toxins. Shop
the perimeter of the grocery store. Read labels. Don't eat heavily processed foods with a shelf life of a millenia that glow in the
dark.

Q. What is a good cooking oil to use in the kitchen? Is margarine better than butter?

A. Not all fats are unhealthy. We need to cut our total fat intake
in half, from 42% of calories to 21%, as our ancestors ate. We
also need to improve the quality of fats consumed. Avoid hydrogenated fats, such as Crisco. Minimize saturated fats, such as
lard and gravies. Butter is better than maragarine. The best oil
to use in the kitchen is olive oil followed by canola oil. Take a
tablespoon each day of one of the following therapeutic oils: cod
liver, flax, borage, evening primrose, or black current seed.

BEVERAGES TO EMPHASIZE

† Purified water
† Cafix
† Roma
† Herb tea
† Vitamin C powder & honey in hot water
† Ginger tea
† Hot natural apple juice with vitamin C
† Fresh orange juice
† Postum
† Chickory
† Japanese Green tea
† Roasted rice or barley tea
† Vinegar, honey & water

DRAGON-SLAYER SHAKE

I don't like taking pills, even when I know the value of using supplements to improve my health. That's why I developed this "shake". While most of us are familiar with milkshakes, there are many variations on that theme which can provide nutrient-dense foods in a convenient format.

The dragon-slayer shake can help make pill taking more tolerable, because the shake lubricates the throat to make pills slide down easier. This shake can be a quick and easy breakfast. Depending on your calorie requirements, use this shake in addition to or instead of the breakfast suggestions listed later. My typical breakfast consists of this Dragon-Slayer shake, whole grain rolls, bagles, muffins or Pita bread, along with a large serving of fresh fruit in season.

Take up to half of your pills with the "Dragon-Slayer shake" and save the remaining pills for later in the day. Taking supplements in small divided dosages helps to maintain sustained levels of nutrients in the bloodstream.

Ingredients:
4-8 ounces of dilute fruit juice, including apple, cranberry, orange, fresh squeezed, juice extracted, etc. I add twice the specified water to a can of frozen unsweetened concentrated apple juice from your grocery store.

1/2 to 1 cup of whole peeled carrots

10-15 grams of powdered protein from (listed in order of preference): whey, rice, soy, alfalfa, egg white, non-fat yogurt solids, spirulina. Do not use powdered proteins that are based upon non-fat milk solids. Too many people are allergic to this product. Your health food store should have a dozen different products to select from.

One sliced ripe banana (preferably frozen). Banana

adds texture via pectin to make this shake have true milk shake viscosity.

1-2 tablespoons of granular lecithin

2-4 grams of vitamin C powder.

1 tablespoon of pure flaxseed oil

1 teaspoon of Lactobacillus acidophilus powder, preferably Natren brand (ph. 800-992-3323)

Directions:

Use a large blender or a Vitamix (1-800-VITAMIX). First puree the carrots in the fruit juice for about 20-30 seconds. Then add the powdered ingredients, followed by the flax oil and finally the frozen banana. Blend until smooth.

BULK COOKING

Yogurt

Scald (foaming but not yet at boiling) 8 cups of milk with one cup of added powder milk.

Turn heat down and simmer for at least 5 minutes; the longer you simmer (up to 25 minutes) the thicker your yogurt will be.

While the milk is simmering, place 2 tablespoons of live cultured good-tasting yogurt in each of two quart-glass peanut butter jars and stir briefly with a plastic spoon until creamy.

After simmering milk, let the temperature drop to 49 degrees C. (112 F.). You don't want to kill the yogurt bacteria with milk that is too hot.

Add about a half cup of the warm milk to the yogurt starter in each of two jars and stir gently but thoroughly. Then add the rest of the milk to the glass jars.

Place the jars (uncovered) in a picnic thermos (the size that holds a six pack of soft drink cans). Close the thermos lid and leave for 6-10 hours. The longer it sits, the thicker it gets. (Do not open container and peek while the fermentation is occurring.)

You can cut the cost of yogurt from $21.00 per gallon to $3 per gallon (cost of milk).

Growing your own Sprouts

You will need a glass jar (quart size or larger), a soft plastic screen for the top, and a rubber band to hold the screen in place. There are also commercial sprouting kits available in most health food stores. Place about one heaping tablespoon of seeds in your glass container with the screen doubled on the top. The seeds will expand about tenfold as they sprout, so allow enough room for their expansion. Fill the container half full of purified water and let stand overnight.

Next morning drain and rinse the seeds. Let stand inverted over the sink for proper drainage. Rinse and drain twice each day for the next 6-7 days. Keep the jar in a dimly lit area.

Larger seeds, like peas, beans, and lentils take a shorter time to grow and should not be allowed to grow more than a half inch long, since they will develop a bitter flavor. Mung bean sprouts can get up to two inches in length without bitter flavor. Wheat, barley, oats, and other grass plants make terrific sprouts. Smaller seeds, like alfalfa, can grow to an inch in length without any bitter flavor. For some extra vitamin A, let the alfalfa sprouts sit in a sunny window for the last day before eating. The green color indicates the welcome addition of chlorophyll, folacin and beta-carotene.

Homemade Mayonnaise
1 egg
1 tsp. prepared mustard
1/2 tsp. salt
3 tbs apple cider
1 cup canola oil

Put the egg, mustard, salt, and 1/2 cup of the oil in the container of an electric blender or food processor. Blend until smooth. Continue blending or processing while adding the remaining oil very slowly in a steady stream into the center of the egg mixture. Use a small rubber spatula to scrape the mayonnaise into a jar. Store covered in the refrigerator. Yields about 2 cups. Note: If the mayonnaise curdles, blend or process 1 egg in the container of a clean electric blender or food processor and gradually pour the curdled mayonnaise back in while blending or processing at high speed.

SPICEY BEANS

3 cups of pinto beans
1 large onion cup up
3-4 garlic cloves minced
2-3 dry red peppers cut up fine
1 tablespoon chili powder
1 tsp cumin powder
1/3 cup olive oil
Lite salt

Sort and wash beans in a colander. Soak the beans overnight in about 8 cups of water in a heavy saucepan. Drain, then fill with another 8 cups of clean water. Add rest of the ingredients. Cover and simmer for 90-120 minutes or until beans are tender. Blend with an egg beater. Add a bit of salt to taste.

If you need the beans sooner:
Rinse beans. Then fill pot with beans and 8 cups of water. Allow to boil for 2 minutes. Let sit in a covered pot for 1 hour. Discard water. Using a pressure cooker, place the soaked and rinsed beans in 5 cups of water

in pot. Add ingredients. Bring lid weight to a gentle rocking motion, then pressure cook for 25 minutes. Let cool down. Beat with a mixer to desired consistency.

BARLEY

Rinse barley and cook for 35-45 minutes in a large volume of boiling water. Barley increases its bulk by four fold when cooked. Drain excess water. Store extra barley in baggies and place in freezer for later use. Season the barley with spices that go with the entree. Spike, Mrs. Dash and other herbal seasonings go with anything.

If using a pressure cooker, use twice the amount of barley measurement for the water. Bring to a rock, then immediately remove from stove burner. Follow rest of the directions .

Better Butter
Blend equal parts of olive or canola oil and softened butter.

Whole Wheat Piecrust
1 cup whole wheat pastry flour
1/2 teaspoon salt
3 tablespoons oil
1/4 cup water

Stir dry ingredients together. Mix in oil. Add enough of the water to make the dough form a ball. Roll flat between sheets of waxed paper and lift into pan.

Make edge.

Roasted Brown Rice or Barley Tea
Dry roast uncooked grain over medium flame for 10 minutes or until a fragrant aroma develops. Stir and shake pan occasionally. Add 2 to 3 tablespoons of the grain to 1 1/2 quarts of purified water. Bring to a boil, simmer 10 to 15 minutes.

The following recipes are not carved in stone. If you do not like a certain spice or seasoning, leave it out. Also, some days you might feel like cooking more than others. These menus were included to provide a wide exposure of different foods and cooking methods. Also, it is a good idea to have leftovers to freeze in serving sizes so you can just pull out easy-to-serve dinners on days you want to relax.

ONE WEEK OF NUTRITIOUS AND DELICIOUS EATING

	Breakfast	Lunch	Dinner
MONDAY	ginger tea, alpine barley, fruit in season	soy pilaf with fruit salad	Baked fish with herbs, fast vegetable soup, evening oats, chocolate cake
TUESDAY	whole wheat english muffin, sesame spread, fruit	linguini, cabbage salad	Baked chicken, yams, California spinach salad, rice porridge
WEDNESDAY	Dragon Slayer drink, toast	pita bread sandwich, onion soup	Turkey loaf, homemade applesauce, sprout salad with peaches and almonds, pita bread, miso dessert balls
THURSDAY	Apple bran muffin, yogurt	Cottage cheese sandwich, fresh piece of fruit	Pressure cooked stew, rye bread, raspberry couscous cake
FRIDAY	Shredded wheat cereal with apple juice, yogurt and fruit	barbeque tempeh, spinach bean sprout salad	salmon patties, fruited rice pilaf, cold Italian veggies, banana pudding.
SATURDAY	Mexican omelete, fruit	tofu steak, fruit, tomato juice	pizza, banana waldorf, Chinese chews
SUNDAY	eggs fried in pam or a bit of butter, Anner's blender pancakes, fruit	humus in pita bread, candy carrots with nuts	turkey, seasoned bulger, orange and onion salad, vanilla yogurt

RECIPES FOR THE WEEK

Monday

Ginger tea
1/2 to 1 teaspoon grated ginger
1/4 teaspoon vitamin C
honey to taste
1 cup hot water
  Mix all ingredients together.

Alpine Barley
2 cups cooked barley
1 tsp. sesame oil
1/4 tsp. ground cumin
1/4 tsp. ground coriander
1/2 tsp. ground cinnamon
1/4 cup golden raisins
1/4 cup dried apricots, chopped
1/2 cup chopped, roasted
almond, walnuts or sunseeds
(optional)
  Cook barley according to directions or use leftovers. Heat oil in pot. Quickly saute spices to bring out their flavors. Add dried fruit and 1 cup water. Cover and simmer 5 minutes. Add cooked barley; heat thoroughly. More water may be needed to reach desired consistency. Serve with chopped nuts.

Soy Pilaf
1/4 cup canola oil or olive oil
1/8 tsp. black pepper
1 bay leaves, crumbled
1 pinch cloves
1/4 tsp cinnamon
1 Tbs. minced fresh onion
1 clove minced garlic
1/2 tsp. grated fresh ginger

1/8 tsp. cayenne
1 cup diced celery
1/2 cup cooked brown rice
1 cup cooked soybeans
  Toast all ingredients, except rice and soybeans. Add grain and beans and then heat. Add vegetable salt or soy sauce to taste.

Fruit Salad
Any fruit in season chopped into bite size pieces and pour vanilla yogurt over the top.

Baked Fish
1 whole fish (salmon, cod, snapper) or piece about 2 1/2 pounds
1/2 cup chopped fresh parsley
2 tablespoons combination of chopped fresh herbs: dill, chives, chervil, basil, sage
1 teaspoon Spike (optional)
1 tablespoon water
1 tablespoon lemon juice

  Place fish on foil. Sprinkle herbs to taste inside cavity. Mix water with lemon juice and sprinkle over outside of fish. Fold foil over and seal.
  Place wrapped fish on baking sheet and bake in 450 degree oven for 10 minutes for every 1 inch thickness of fish, plus an additional 10 minutes cooking time because it's wrapped in foil

(35 to 40 minutes total cooking time), or until fish is opaque. Unwrap and discard skin; most of it should stick to foil. Place fish on warmed platter. Garnish with parsley, dill, or watercress if you'd like.

Fast Vegetable Soup
2 cups skim milk (or a milk substitute from soy or rice)
1 tablespoon butter or "better butter"
2 tablespoon whole wheat flour
2 teaspoons Gayelord's all natural vegetable broth
1 teaspoon Spike
1/4 teaspoon pepper (optional)
2 cups cooked vegetables

Put all ingredients in blender in order listed. Cover and blend until smooth. Pour into a saucepan. Cook, stirring occasionally, over low heat until hot.

Evening Oats
1 small to medium apple chopped
1 tbs. butter
1 1/2 cup uncooked oats
1 egg beaten
1/2 cup water
1-2 tbs. honey
1 tsp. cinnamon
1/4 tsp. salt
1/2 tsp vanilla

Saute the apple bits in butter

in a skillet. Combine oats and egg in a bowl. Mix. Add oats to apples. Cook over medium heat 3 to 5 minutes, stirring until oats are dry and lightly brown. Add remaining ingredients. Continue cooking, stirring occasionally until liquid evaporates-about 3 minutes. Makes 2 cups.

Chocolate Cake
Whole Wheat Cake bottom:
1/3 cup honey
1/4 cup butter softened
1 egg
2/3 cup yogurt
1-2 tsp. vanilla
1/2 tsp. almond extract (optional)
1 cup whole wheat flour
1 1/2 tsp. baking powder
14 tsp. salt

Cream together honey and butter; add egg, yogurt, and vanilla. Stir. Add remaining ingredients stirring until smootlh. Pour batter into greased 8 or 9 inch round baking dish. Heat 10 minutes on power level 7 or medium in microwave. Let stand, covered, 10 minutes. Store covered until cool.

Chocolate Frosting
1/4 cup butter softened
1/4 cup honey
1-2 teaspoon vanilla
1/2 cup yogurt
3 tablespoons cocoa powder

3 tablespoons carob powder (or a total of 6 tablespoons cocoa powder if you don't want to use carob)
dash of salt (optional)
1/4 cup chopped nuts (optional)
About 1 1/2 cups dry non-fat milk powder (or whey milk substitute)
dry pectin or powdered sugar (optional) for thickener

Mix first 4 ingredients until smooth. Stir in cocoa and carob. Sift or stir in the powder milk. Will be slightly lumpy if just stirred. Mix until slightly runny. Taste to see if mixture needs to be sweeter. Can add powder sugar. The frosting tends to thicken up, so wait a few minutes before frosting the cake for the right consistency. Sprinkle with nuts. Keep in refrigerator. Frosts 2 single layer cakes.

Tuesday

Sesame Spread
3/4 cup sesame seeds
1 tablespoon honey
1/4 cup apple juice or water
1/8 teaspoon salt

Toast sesame seeds and grind into a meal in a blender. Remove to a bowl and add honey, water, and salt. The mixture will thicken as it cools, so you may want to thin it by adding more juice.

Linguini
1/2 pound whole wheat linguini or any other whole wheat noodle
1 tablespoon olive oil
1 clove garlic, minced
1/2 cup finely diced mushrooms
1/3 cup minced fresh parsley
1/4 cup grated soy cheese
Lite Salt or salt substitute to taste

Bring 2 quarts of water to a boil in a medium size saucepan. Add the noodles and cook for about 5 minutes. Drain thoroughly. Immediately return the pot to the stove and add the olive oil, garlic, and mushrooms. Cook for 3 minutes over medium heat. Add the drained noodles and parsley, and toss. Add the cheese and salt to taste and toss again.

Cabbage Salad
1/4 of a head of a medium cabbage
2 carrots
1 diced onion (small)
raisins
sunflower seeds
Italian dressing

Grate cabbage and carrots. Add onion, raisins and sunflower seeds to taste. Sprinkle with Italian dressing.
Variation: Add any of the following: diced prunes, diced apples, walnuts, pecans, bell peppers, any other vegetables or dried fruit.

Baked Chicken and Yams
4 pieces of chicken
4 baking yams (medium size)

Wash chicken and place in oven-proof pan with enough room so the pieces aren't crowded. Scrub yams and poke with a knife several times. Place chicken and yams in oven and cook at 375 F. for 45 to 50 minutes.

California Spinach Salad
4 cups torn spinach leaves
1-2 cups alfalfa sprouts
1/4 pound mushrooms, sliced
1 large tomato, cut in chunks
2 spring onions, chopped
Toss ingredients together. Serve with Avocado dressing or your favorite.

Avocado Dressing
1/2 large ripe avocado
1 tablespoon lemon juice
1/8 teaspoon salt
1/8 teaspoon chili powder
squeezed garlic
1/4 cup buttermilk (or milk substitute)
Mix all ingredients well. Serve over salad.

Rice Porridge
1 cup cooked brown rice, cold
1/2 cup apple juice
1/2 cup water
2 Tbs. raisins or other dried fruit
1/2 tsp. cinnamon (opt.)
2 Tbs. chopped nuts (opt.)
Place all ingredients in a saucepan. Bring to a boil, then reduce heat and simmer, covered, 15 minutes stirring frequently. Most of the liquid should be absorbed. Serve warm. If creamier porridge is desired, puree half.

Wednesday

Pita Bread Sandwich
You can create your own with: cheese, tomato, sprouts, garbanzo beans, grated carrot, sunflower seeds with Italian dressing

Onion Soup
1/2 to 1 tablespoon canola or
  sesame oil
  2 lb. onions, thinly sliced
  2 cloves garlic crushed
    1/2-1 qt. stock
    (Gayelord's vegetable
    broth)
    1-2 tablespoon miso
    1/4 cup chopped celery
    leaves (optional)
2 teaspoons molasses
1-2 teaspoons Spike

Saute onions and garlic in butter over medium heat in a large saucepan for about 10 minutes. Add the rest of the ingredients and bring to a boil. Reduce heat and simmer for 5 to 10 minutes. Can serve with croutons.

Turkey Meat Loaf
1 pound extra lean ground turkey
1 large onion, finely chopped
1/4 cup natural bran

1 slice whole wheat bread, crumbled (or 1/2 cup Rice crispies)
1/2 teaspoon thyme
1 teaspoon Spike
dash of Worcestershire sauce
1 cup tomato juice or tomato sauce
1 egg, lightly beaten
1 tablespoon chopped fresh herbs-thyme, rosemary, savory, sage, parsley (optional)

In a mixing bowl, combine all ingredients. Turn into 9x5-inch loaf pan or baking dish. Bake in 350 degree oven for 45 minutes, or until brown and firm to the touch.

Homemade Applesauce
6 apples
handful raisins
1/2 cup water or apple juice
honey to taste
1/2 teaspoon cinnamon
1/4 teaspoon nutmeg
1/4 teaspoon allspice
1/4 teaspoon cloves

Core apples and cut into chunks. Add remaining ingredients including enough honey to sweeten to taste. Bring to a boil and then simmer until tender. Mash with a fork or potato masher. Lemon lends a nice bit of zip to the flavor.

Sprout Salad with Peaches
sprouts
peaches
almond slices

On a bed of sprouts, add some peaches with their juice. Sprinkle a few almond slices on top.

Miso Dessert Balls
1/2 cup peanut butter
1/2 cup honey
1/4 cup carob powder
1/4 cup milk powder (or milk substitute whey powder)
1/4 cup wheat germ
1/4 cup chopped almonds
1/4 cup sunflower seeds
1 1/2 teaspoon miso
1/2 teaspoon cinnamon

Combine all ingredients and mix thoroughly. Roll into bite size balls. Refrigerate.

Thursday

Apple Bran Muffin
1 cup whole wheat flour
3/4 cup wheat bran
1/4 teaspoon salt
1/2 teaspoon baking soda
1/4 teaspoon nutmeg
1/4 teaspoon cinnamon
1/2 cup finely chopped apple
1/4 cup raisins
1/4 cup chopped nuts
1 cup buttermilk
1 beaten egg
1/4 cup molasses
1 tablespoon oil
1/2 teaspoon maple flavor

Preheat oven to 350 degrees. Grease a 12-cup muffin pan.

Toss flour, bran, salt, soda, nut-meg cinnamon together with a fork.

Stir in apples, raisins, and nuts. Combine the liquid ingredients. Stir the liquid ingredients into the dry with a few swift strokes. Pour into greased muffin cups, filling them at least 2/3 full, and bake for 25 minutes. Makes 12.

Cottage Cheese Sandwich

1/2 cup creamed cottage cheese
1/6 cup wheat germ
1/2 tbs. green chillies
1/8 tsp. oregano leaves
1/8 tsp. basil leaves
2 tsp. finely chopped onion
dash salt
dash tabasco (optional)
tomato slices
alfalfa sprouts

Mix first 8 ingredients together well. Put mound of mixture on a slice of whole wheat bread or toast. Top with a tomato slice and sprouts. Can have an open face sandwich or closed.

Pressure Cooked Stew

1 pound lean lamb, cut into 1-inch cubes
1 tablespoon olive oil
3 cups water with vegetable broth added
1 large diced potato
2 medium diced carrots
1 onion diced
3 cloves garlic crushed
1 bay leaf

1 teaspoon soy sauce
1/4 cup worcestershire
2 tablespoons whole wheat flour
1/2 cup cold water

Shake the 1/2 cup cold water and flour in tightly covered container. Set aside. Cook and stir meat in olive oil in a pressure cooker until meat is browned, about 15 minutes. Add the water. Pressure cook by bringing it to a rock and let it gently rock for 30 minutes. Take off heat. Let off steam properly. Add the rest of the ingredients and let it get back to a rock for 7 minutes. Remove from heat. Let off steam properly. Stir in the flour mixture. You can use a strainer to remove any lumps. Bring to a boil. Serves 5 or 6.

Raspberry Couscous Cake

2 cups couscous
pinch sea salt
5 cups apple juice
1 lemon, grated rind and juice
1 pint raspberries

Bring apple juice and sea salt to a boil in a saucepan; then add lemon rind and juice. Add couscous; lower heat and stir until almost thick. Remove from stove; stir in washed berries. Pour cake into glass baking dish that has been lightly sprayed with lecithin oil (Pam). Allow to cool and cut into squares. Garnish with roasted nuts or fruit sauce.

Friday

Barbeque Tempeh
1 lb. tempeh
2 Tbs. mustard
2 Tbs. miso
water to cover

Cut tempeh in "burger-size" portions. Place in a pot and cover with water. Dissolve miso and mustard in 1/4 cup water; then add to tempeh and bring to a boil. Lower heat and simmer for 20 minutes. Remove from liquid. Place in frying pan with sauce and use sauce to baste. Cook 5 to 10 minutes on each side. Serve on whole wheat bun or roll, with sliced onion, lettuce and sprouts.

Sauce:
1/2 cup apple juice
1 Tbs. soy sauce
1/2 Tbs. lemon juice
1/2 Tbs. rice syrup (opt.)
1 small piece ginger root, grated
1 tsp arrowroot dissolved in a little water

Place apple juice, soy sauce and syrup in a small saucepan. Simmer gently on a low heat to reduce volume slightly. Thicken with arrowroot. Add ginger. Adjust flavor.

Spinach & Bean sprout Salad
8 ounces spinach
16 ounces bean sprouts or alfalfa sprouts
croutons (optional)

Sesame Dressing
1/4 cup soy sauce
2 tablespoons toasted sesame seeds
2 tablespoon finely chopped onion
1/2 teaspoon honey
1/4 teaspoon pepper

Mix all ingredients.

Variations:
† grated carrots
† grated cheese
† cooked noodles
† diced egg
† chopped apples
† cut up dried fruit
† avocado
† nuts
† onions
† crushed bacon
† tomatoes
† any vegetables

Salmon Patties

1 can salmon
2/3 cup old fashion oatmeal cereal, uncooked
1 Tbs lemon juice
1 tsp. dried parsley flakes
2 eggs

Remove the skin from the salmon but leave the bones if you want the extra calcium. Mix with the rest of the ingredients.

Make into patties. Fry in a bit of olive oil until brown on both sides.

Fruited Bulger Pilaf
1 tablespoon "better butter"
1 medium onion chopped
1 cup bulger uncooked
1/4 teaspoon dill weed
1/4 teaspoon oregano
1/2 teaspoon salt (optional)
1/4 teaspoon pepper
1 tablespoon parsley chopped
chopped apricots, dates and raisins to taste
2 cups water with 1 tablespoon miso mixed in it

Melt butter in large skillet. Add bulger and vegetables. Stir constantly until vegetables are tender and bulger is golden. Add the rest of the ingredients. Bring to a boil. Stir. Reduce heat and simmer 15 minutes.

Italian Cold Vegetables
Using up leftover vegetables (i.e. broccoli, cauliflower, Chile peppers, mushrooms, carrots, zuccini, all beans). Just make sure they haven't been over-cooked.
Sprinkle with small amount of marinade from:
1/2 cup olive oil
1/2 cup apple cider vinegar
1/2 tsp. basil
1/2 tsp. oregano leaves
1/2 chopped onion
1 chopped clove garlic
1/4 tsp. sea salt

1/2 tsp dry mustard
1 tsp. paprika
1 tbs. honey

Banana Pudding
5 ripe bananas
4 oz low fat cream cheese
3/4 cup yogurt
1 tsp. vanilla
2 tbs. lemon juice

Blend all ingredients. Chill.

Saturday

Mexican Omelet
3 eggs scrambled
salsa
grated cheese (optional)

Spray Pam in a frying pan. Add the scrambled eggs. Cover and cook over medium low heat until almost set. Flip. Add salsa to top of eggs and spread. Can add a bit of grated cheese. Put cover back on. Finish cooking. Remove lid. Fold the omelet in half.

Textured Tofu
The day before, slice firm tofu and pat dry. Freeze separately. Drop frozen tofu into boiling water. Take out when it's been defrosted. When cool enough to touch, ring out and pat dry. Set aside.

Tofu Steak
In a baggie, add:
1/4 cup water

1 teaspoon vegetable broth
dash Spike
dash poultry seasoning

Add tofu to baggie and marinade. Dip tofu in a beaten egg. Then bread in equal parts of whole wheat flour and corn meal. Fry in small amount of olive oil.

Pizza

Pizza Topping
1 pound ripe tomatoes, blanched, seeded,chopped, and drained as much as possible
Lite Salt & pepper
4 ounces soy cheese, thinly sliced
1 teaspoon dried basil
1/2 teaspoon oregano
1/2 teaspoon parsley
1 onion sliced fine
mushrooms sliced fine (opt.)
4 tablespoon Parmeson cheese
1 tablespoon olive oil

Prepare the pizza dough. Spread the tomatoes almost to the edge, and season well. Cover with the thinly sliced mozzarella; onions, mushrooms, then top with the basil, parsley, oregano, and Parmesan cheese. Sprinkle a little olive oil over the top, and place in a preheated hot oven (450 degrees) for 20 minutes, or until the dough has cooked through and the cheese has melted. Serve.

Pizza Dough
1/2 tablespoon dried yeast

1/2 teaspoon sucanat (sugar cane)
2/3 cup warm water
2 cups whole wheat flour
1 teaspoon Lite Salt
2 tablespoon olive oil

Dissolve yeast with the sugar in 3 to 4 tablespoons of warm water. Leave for 5 to 10 minutes in a warm place (until frothy). Put the flour and salt into a warm bowl; make a well in the center, and pour in the yeast mixture, water, and oil. Mix until it forms a soft dough, adding a bit of warm water if necessary. Turn out onto a floured surface, and knead well for about 5 minutes. Place dough in a floured bowl and cover with a damp cloth. Leave in a warm place until it doubles -about 1 1/2 to 2 hours. Knead lightly. Roll out or press into a pizza pan or baking tray. Pat gently so it fits,with the edges a bit higher.

Banana Waldorf
2 cups diced banana
1 1/2 cups diced apple
1 cup diced celery
1/2 cup chopped walnuts
1/2 cup raisins
1/2 cup yogurt
1 tablespoon lemon juice

Use well-chilled fruit. Combine all ingredients. Mix well and serve on top of fresh spinach leaves or alfalfa sprouts. Yields 6 small servings.

Chinese Chews
1/4 cup butter
1 1/2 cups hulled sesame seeds
(or: 3/4 cup sesame seeds, 1/4
crushed almonds, 1/4 cup
coconut)
3/4 cup dry milk (or whey milk
substitute)
1/6 cup wheat germ
1/2 cup honey
1 to 2 tsp. vanilla
2 tsp. brewers yeast (optional)

Melt butter in skillet. Add sesame seeds and lightly toast, stirring often. Stir in powder milk and wheat germ. Add honey and vanilla mixing well. Continue to cook for about 7 to 8 minutes, stirring constantly. Scoop and press lightly into a greased cookie sheet. Cool and cut into squares.

Sunday

Anner's Blender Pancakes
1 ripe banana
1 egg
1/2 cup flour (wheat, oat, buck-wheat)
2 teaspoon baking powder (without alum as an ingredient)
1/2 teaspoon maple flavoring (optional)

Blend the banana, egg, and flavoring in a blender. Add the dry ingredients. Fry as normal in Pam; covering the pan while cooking on the first side.

Humus
1/2 onion, chopped
1 clove garlic crushed
1 tablespoon olive oil
dash cummin
1 teaspoon basil
1/2 teaspoon oregano
2 tablespoon parsley, chopped fine
juice of 1 lemon
1/4 cup sesame seed butter tahini (optional)
3 cups cooked garbanzo beans, mashed
salt to taste

Saute onion and garlic in oil until onion is transparent. Add cumin and cook until fragrant. Add herbs at the last moment, cooking just enough to soften parsley. Mix with the lemon and mashed beans and tahini, stirring together thoroughly. Makes about 3 cups.

Candy Carrots
1/2 pound fresh carrots
honey
chopped almonds

Cut carrots into 2 1/2x1/4 - inch strips. Place carrots in a microwave bowl. Drizzle honey over top. Sprinkle almonds. Cook on high for about 6 minutes in the microwave.

No Fuss Turkey

Clean turkey. Place in a turkey pan. Spread a bit of canola oil over the top and cover tightly with lid or foil. Cook turkey for the amount of time needed based upon the weight of the bird.

Seasoned Bulger

To 3 cups cooked bulger, add:
1 1/2 tablespoon vegetable broth
raisins
sunflower seeds
2 teaspoons Spike

Mix together and warm in the microwave.

Orange and Onion Salad

2 oranges
1 diced avocado (optional)
1 grapefruit
1 small red onion, thinly sliced
and separated into rings
1/3 cup yogurt
2 tablespoons chopped walnuts
(optional)
salad greens or spinach leaves
salt and pepper to taste

Peel and section the fruit. Cut each section into two or three pieces and put in a salad bowl. Add all the juices from the oranges and grapefruit to the onion. Add avocado. Pour yogurt over mixture, toss and chill. Sprinkle with nuts, salt and pepper and serve on salad greens.

APPENDIX

◆

BIBLES USED:

AMPLIFIED BIBLE, Zondervan Publishing, Grand Rapids, MI, 1987

RYRIE STUDY BIBLE, New International Version, Moody Press, Chicago, 1994

THOMPSON CHAIN HYPERBIBLE, New International Version, for MacIntosh computers, version 2.5, Beacon Technologies, 1993

HEALTH AND BIBLE BOOKS:

Wade, C., *THE MIRACLE OF BIBLE HEALING FOODS*, Globe Communications Corp., Boca Raton, FL, 1991

Kroeger, H., *GOD HELPS THOSE THAT HELP THEMSELVES*, 1984

Ward, B., *HEALING FOODS FROM THE BIBLE*, Globe Communications, Boca Raton, FL 1994

Kloss, J., *BACK TO EDEN*, Back to Eden Books Publishing, Loma Linda, CA, 1972

Skarin, A., *THE BOOK OF BOOKS*, DeVorss & Co., Publishers, Marina del Rey, CA 1972

Jafolla, R & M., *NOURISHING THE LIFE FORCE*, Unity Village, MS, 1983

Treben, M ., *HEALTH THROUGH GOD'S PHARMACY*, Wilhelm Ennsthaler, Austria, 1980

McMillen, S.I., *NONE OF THESE DISEASES*, Fleming H. Revell, Grand Rapids, MI,1984

GOOD NUTRITION REFERENCES:

Anderson, *WELLNESS MEDICINE*, Keats, 1987
Balch & Balch, *PRESCRIPTION FOR NUTRITIONAL HEALING*, Avery, 1993
Eaton, *PALEOLITHIC PRESCRIPTION*, Harper & Row, 1988
Grabowski, RJ, *CURRENT NUTRITIONAL THERAPY*, Image Press, 1993
Haas, *STAYING HEALTHY WITH NUTRITION*, Celestial, 1992
Hausman, *THE RIGHT DOSE*, Rodale, 1987
Hendler, *DOCTOR'S VITAMIN AND MINERAL ENCYCLOPE- DIA*, Simon & Schuster,1990
Lieberman, *REAL VITAMIN & MINERAL BOOK*, Avery, 1990
Murray, *ENCYCLOPEDIA OF NATURAL MEDICINE*, Prima, 1990
National Research Council, *RECOMMENDED DIETARY ALLOWANCES*, National Academy Press, 1989
Price, *NUTRITION AND PHYSICAL DEGENERATION*, Keats, 1989
Quillin, *HEALING NUTRIENTS*, Random House, 1987
Shils, *MODERN NUTRITION IN HEALTH & DISEASE*, Lea & Febiger, 1994
Werbach, *NUTRITIONAL INFLUENCES ON ILLNESS*, Third Line, 1993

WHERE TO BUY NUTRITION PRODUCTS BY MAIL ORDER

BULK FOODS

Allergy Resources Inc., 195 Huntington Beach Dr., Colorado Springs, CO 80921, ph. 719-488-3630
Deer Valley Farm, RD#1, Guilford, NY 13780, ph. 607-674-8556
Diamond K Enterprises, Jack Kranz, R.R. 1, Box 30, St. Charles, MN 55972, ph. 507-932-4308

Gravelly Ridge Farms, Star Route 16, Elk Creek, CA 95939, ph. 916-963-3216

Green Earth, 2545 Prairie St., Evanston, IL 60201, ph. 800-322-3662

Healthfoods Express, 181 Sylmar Clovis, CA 93612, ph. 209-252-8321

Jaffe Bros. Inc., PO Box 636, Valley Center, CA 92082, ph. 619-749-1133

Macrobiotic Wholesale Co., 799 Old Leicester Hwy, Asheville, NC 28806, ph. 704-252-1221

Moksha Natural Foods, 724 Palm Ave., Watsonville, CA, 95076, ph. 408-724-2009

Mountain Ark Co., 120 South East Ave., Fayetteville, AR, 72701, ph. 501-442-7191, or 800-643-8909

New American Food Co., PO Box 3206, Durham, NC 27705, ph. 919-682-9210

Timber Crest Farms, 4791 Dry Creek, Healdsburg, CA, 95448, ph. 707-433-8251, FAX -8255

Walnut Acres, Walnut Acres Road, Penns Creek, PA 17862, ph. 717-837-0601

LARGE STORES THAT SELL VITAMINS, MINERALS, & SOME HERBS BY MAIL
Bronson, 800-235-3200
NutriGuard, 800-433-2402
Health Center for Better Living, 813-566-2611
Vitamin Research Products, 800-877-2447
Vitamin Trader, 800-334-9310
Terrace International, 800-824-2434
Willner Chemists, 800-633-1106
Progressive Labs, 800-527-9512

STORES THAT SPECIALIZE IN SELLING HERBS BY MAIL
Gaia Herbals, 800-994-9355
Frontier Herbs 800-786-1388; fax 319-227-7966
Blessed Herbs 800-489-HERB; fax 508-882-3755
Trout Lake Farm 509-395-2025

San Francisco Herb Co. fax 800-227-5430
Star West 800-800-4372

RECOMMENDED COOKBOOKS

Kathy Cooks Naturally, Kathy Hoshijo
Super Seafood, Tom Ney
Eat Well, Live Well, Pamela Smith
Natural Foods Cookbook, Mary Estella
American Cancer Society Cookbook, Anne Lindsay
Mix & Match Cooking for Health, Jennie Shapter
The Healthy Gourmet Cookbook, Barbara Bassett
How to Use Natural Foods Deliciously, Barbara Bassett
The "I Can't Believe This Has No Sugar" Cookbook,
Deborah Buhr
Eat Smart for a Healthy Heart Cookbook, Dr. Denton Cooley &
Dr. Carolyn Moore
Simply Light Cooking, Kitchens of Weight Watchers
Healthy Life-Style Cookbook, Weight Watchers
The American Health Food Book, Robert Barnett, Nao Hauser
The Chez Eddy Living Heart Cookbook, Antonio Gotto Jr.

REFERENCES

Chapter 1
1. Price, WA, *NUTRITION AND PHYSICAL DEGENERATION*, Keats, New Canaan, 1945
2. Eaton, SB, et al., *PALEOLITHIC PRESCRIPTION*, Harper, NY, 1988
3. McMillen, SI, *NONE OF THESE DISEASES*, p.90, Baker, Grand Rapids, 1984

Chapter 2
1. Braunwald, E., *New England Journal Medicine*, vol.309, p.1181, Nov.10, 1983
2. Le, MG, et al., *Journal of the National Cancer Institute*, vol.77, p.633, 1986

INDEX

---◆---